LESSONS
FROM AN
IMPERFECT
WORLD

LESSONS
FROM AN
IMPERFECT
WORLD

Stories that inspire, give hope and speak from the heart

HARRY J. GRETHER

With my best wishes - Harry Grether

RSVP
RISING SUN VENTURE PRODUCTIONS, LLC

Rising Sun Venture Productions, LLC
Midland, Michigan

LESSONS FROM AN IMPERFECT WORLD
by Harry Grether

First Edition.

ISBN 0-9766675-0-9

Published by RSVP
Rising Sun Venture Productions, LLC
P.O. Box 1295
Midland, Michigan 48641-1295

Visit Harry Grether at www.harrygrether.com

The ideas and suggestions in this book should by no means be considered a substitute for the advice of a qualified professional. Neither the author nor the publisher are engaged in rendering any professional services or advice to the individual reader, nor shall they be held liable for any adverse effects arising from information contained in this book.

The names and identifying characteristics of several people in the stories in this book have been changed to protect their privacy and dignity.

This book may be purchased at quantity discounts for educational, business, or other promotional purposes. Contact Rising Sun Venture Productions, P.O. Box 1295, Midland, MI 48641-1295.

Twenty percent of all profits from this book and related speaking engagements will be donated to assist one or more of the following: hospice, the hungry, homeless, elderly, or disabled.

THIS BOOK IS DEDICATED
WITH LOVE AND AFFECTION TO:

…my daughter Sheri
a daughter every father would be proud of having.
You are a terrific mom and teacher.
Your energy, compassion and love seem endless.

…my daughter Denise
who now lives in the perfect world.
You taught me so much about life and death
and also about courage and love.

…my wife, Helen
for your understanding and unwavering love and support.
You are the wind beneath my wings.

…my mother, Emy
for your guidance and strength,
as well as your example of patience and compassion.

Contents

ACKNOWLEDGMENTS

The writing of this book has been a new and wonderful experience for me. It has also been one of the most difficult challenges I have ever undertaken. It would be hard to recall the number of times I felt like simply dropping the whole idea. Many special people have shown an interest and provided support and encouragement along the way.

While working on this book, I have been reminded of the many wonderful people who have been a part of my life, and I have also made many new friends. I treasure both.

My deepest gratitude goes to each of the following for their many unique contributions to the creation of this book:

To my wife, Helen, for your love, support, and belief in me, and for letting me follow this dream.

To my daughter, Sheri, and son-in-law, David, for your help, encouragement, and love.

To my wonderful grandchildren, Dima, Alex, and Nadya for your contributions and for the inspiration you have provided me through your imaginations and creativity.

To Gregg White for your help and encouragement. You have been a special person in my life.

To Rich Baldwin, a talented author, wise mentor, and wonderful friend. Without your knowledge and patience, this book would not have been completed.

To Matt and Lucy Kiss for telling your wonderful story and for allowing me to share it in this book. Your friendship is a gift I am thankful for.

To Father Bob Malloy for your assistance and support and for being so generous with your time. Your knowledge and insights have meant a great deal to me, and your unselfish service has aided hundreds of people in need.

To Sarah Thomas for your exceptional talents in cover design and text layout.

To Anne Ordiway, Joyce Wagner, and Gail Garber for your skillful editing and proofreading. And to Sam Nesbitt for your interest and support.

To Elon Basgall for your constant enthusiastic support and also for introducing me to the important world of hospice. Your belief in me has helped to keep this ship afloat.

To Penny Rowles for your interest in my hospice work and in this book. Your encouragement and friendship are important to me.

To Julie Luginbill and Ellie Garrett for the wonderful work you do for hospice, the help and support you have given me, and for your friendship, which I value very much.

To Don and Jan Carlsen for the interest you have shown in my work, the positive influence you have been, and our truly authentic friendship, which has grown from the day we met.

To Sheryl Cergnul, Barbara Warren, John Bretschneider, Al Arens, Pete Barton, Arselia and Al Ensign, and Brian Kroll, you have challenged me, supported me, advised me, and motivated me in ways that have been important and unwavering.

And to the very extraordinary staff at the Grace A. Dow Memorial Library. This wonderful facility has been my second home for the past few years. Not only have the finest resources been available, but the staff has been simply superb; they are

Patty Wilke, you have always been most cooperative, helpful, and always very pleasant to work with.

Ann Jarvis, you are always ready for my questions and you pleasantly take on a challenge.

Suzanna McArdle, your help and your great sense of humor were always welcome when I needed a break or felt a bit discouraged.

Vicki Carto, your constant encouragement as well as your wise counsel and great ideas have been very valuable to me.

Rebecca Hastings, Char Tabor, Deborah Haskin, and Carrie Mac-Donald, you have all been a great help on so many occasions. Also, Jan Zileski at the Cup and Chaucer coffee shop, thank you for your support and for being a great listener.

Melissa Barnard, Library Director; Virginia McKane, Assistant Director; and Carol Souchock, Supervisor of Adult Services, all of you do a fine job of administering an excellent library. Thank you for your help in reaching my goal.

To all of you who in any way contributed to my stories, I hope I have done you justice.

And finally, to anyone I may have forgotten, please forgive me and accept my sincere appreciation.

All of you have influenced my life and made it better.

"How far you go in life depends on your being tender with the young, compassionate with the aged, sympathetic with the striving and tolerant of the weak and strong. Because someday in your life you will have been all of these."

— *George Washington Carver*

...personal note

I have thought about writing this book for quite some time. I do not intend it to be a literary or scholarly piece of work filled with research and data; instead, I simply want to share stories from my own personal experience and a few from others I have had the privilege of meeting along the way. These people and experiences played an important role in shaping my life, and such stories have a powerful way of passing along what we have learned. They refresh the spirit and define the special times in our lives.

With each year, our lives become filled with new experiences. Life may move fairly smoothly for us most of the time, but it also has its highs and lows. We may enjoy wonderful, joyous occasions, such as the birth of a child or the wedding of someone close. We celebrate these times and mark them in our memories. But we will also be confronted with numerous difficult times. To endure and survive these times, it is critical that we have the necessary skills to weather the storm as well as the support of others. All of us will, at some point, face events over which we have absolutely no control. Sometimes, life simply is not fair. This is not a perfect world, yet much in this life is excellent and even awesome.

I share these true stories because they are lessons I have learned along my journey. Some involve everyday experiences to which many of you will relate, while others are more unusual. Each person will find different meaning in the stories based upon his or her own experiences.

We are not alone as we travel life's journey with its good and bad times, for in many ways, our lives are more similar than they are different. The events in our lives may not make history, but they are powerful influences on our own personal growth and memory. Our experiences help us grow, learn, understand, and mature. Through them, we become wiser and more tolerant. They shape our lives.

Thank you for reading my stories. Enjoy!

"A person without a sense of humor is like a wagon without springs, jolted by every pebble in the road."

— Henry Ward Beecher

...about laughter

Halfway into our dinner meal, everyone at our table burst into laughter, attracting the attention of the other people in the large dining room. Rob had just told another of his very funny stories to which we always listened attentively. Not only did we welcome the humor that Rob brought to our meals, but on this occasion, twelve-year-old Billy had just taken a mouthful of mashed potatoes as Rob delivered the punch line to his story. You can picture the rest.

I have never forgotten that summer many years ago when I had the wonderful experience of being a camp counselor in a camp for young people with disabilities. For six weeks, another counselor and I were responsible for cabin #7 at a camp in a beautiful, wooded setting in Michigan. The camp served sixty-four young people, each with a physical disability. The group was split evenly between boys and girls.

A counselor's responsibility included assisting the campers with the daily living tasks they could not handle on their own as well as seeing that they attended and participated in the daily schedule of activities. Needless to say, at times this was a difficult and even a stressful responsibility. The entire six-week camp experience, however, was as enjoyable and productive for me as it was for any of the campers.

Cottages #1 through #4 were for the girls, and #5 through #8 were for the boys. Each cabin had two counselors and eight campers. Four of the campers in our cabin were young men who were either deaf or hard of hearing. My counselor teammate, Al, knew sign language, so he was their counselor. Signing for them, he assisted them throughout all of their daily activities. I was responsible for the other four boys. Mark and Billy had cerebral palsy, and Rob and Dan were dealing with advanced stages of muscular dystrophy. Three of the four were in wheelchairs. With the exception of a few short breaks, I spent the next six weeks, twenty-four hours a day, living with these young men. Needless to say, we got to know each other very well.

Rob and Dan were brothers and were the oldest campers in cabin # 7, being nineteen and seventeen respectively. They each had the most wonderful sense of humor I have ever seen in teenagers. We could count on a humorous performance from Rob or his brother, not only at dinner, but at anytime throughout their waking hours.

Both brothers had been diagnosed with muscular dystrophy early in life and had been able to walk quite well until their early teens. However, since muscular dystrophy is a progressive, degenerative disease, it had

"We could count on a humorous performance from Rob or his brother anytime throughout their waking hours."

become increasingly difficult for the boys to walk in recent years. Eventually, they needed to use braces, crutches, and walkers in order to walk. Then at age seventeen, Rob was fitted for a wheelchair. Four months before camp, Dan also became wheelchair bound. It was difficult for them to watch their muscular functions slip away and know they were becoming more and more dependent on others. Their overall prognosis was not promising.

In spite of all this, Rob and Dan had decided to press on in a determined and positive manner and enjoy life to its fullest. It was a real joy to observe them as they interacted with other campers and staff. Their antics and humor were contagious throughout their daily activities. At archery, they asked if we could make paper targets that resembled the rear ends of donkeys and put tails on them, rather than use the traditional targets. They both enjoyed swimming tremendously. Even with their special flotation devices and the limited use of their legs, they were able to splash and sometimes dunk the other campers and counselors. Fishing off the dock offered them great opportunities to tell fish stories, the likes of which I have not heard since. And, of course, the weekly dances gave the brothers another chance to carry on. Their wheelchairs did not stop them from dancing. The counselors would use one hand to hold hands with them and use the other to guide their wheelchairs. In this way, they would be able to move the wheelchairs around the floor and dance together.

"Their wheelchairs did not stop them from dancing."

Both Rob and Dan were bright young men. They were still attending high school and doing well academically. Though they were becoming more and more limited in what they could do physically, they read and studied, putting their sharp minds and good memories to use by doing something they could still do well. They even brought books to camp with them.

"I am certain that their stories were often made up, but they were always creative and humorous."

After dark on most evenings, all the campers and counselors would gather under the stars and bright moon around a large campfire. After singing and getting our usual fill of s'mores, it was time for a little competition between the cabins. As a team, campers from each of the cabins would tell a scary story, a humorous story, or a joke. At the end, the counselors would vote for the cabin that did the best job. Our cabin won many times, thanks to major contributions from Rob and Dan. The jokes were always in good taste, and the boys were careful not to offend anyone. I am certain that their stories were often made up, but they were always creative and humorous. Both the campers and staff enjoyed the evenings very much.

In early August, when the camping experience ended, it was quite a scene seeing the campers tell each other good-bye. Many of them planned to return the following summer for another fun and memorable time.

The staff also found it difficult to see the summer end. It had been a great learning experience, and we had all made many new friends. However, since most of the staff would not be returning the next year, these would be final good-byes for many of the campers and staff.

As I said goodbye to Rob and Dan, I promised them that I would visit them once or twice during the coming year. Because of family conditions and their ever-increasing need for care, the boys now lived in a nursing home. They were the youngest residents at the home. The boys continued to make me laugh each time I visited them. Within the next two years, Rob passed away; Dan died less than two months after his brother.

"The boys continued to make me laugh each time I visited them."

I was curious to learn how well Rob and Dan had adapted to nursing home life and how well they had been received by the staff and other residents. Margaret, one of the nurses at the home, shared her thoughts with me.

With tears in her eyes, she said, "Those boys brought life into this place the day they moved in. They cared a great deal about the other residents and visited them often. But most of all, their sense of humor was a blessing to all of us. They were always telling stories and jokes. They were always in good taste, and they made us laugh so hard tears came to our eyes. And they loved to play little practical jokes on residents and staff. They were simply a joy to have with us." Margaret ended by saying, "Nothing can ever replace what they gave us."

"Those boys brought life into this place the day they moved in ...Nothing can ever replace what they gave us."

What Margaret said about Rob and Dan sounded familiar. It was really not a surprise to me. They were two young men who cared more about others than about themselves. In spite of their own situations, they made an effort each day to bring some sunshine into the lives of others.

———◁◆▷———

Certainly, the brief number of years that Rob and Dan lived is no measure of their success or contribution to others. Humor and laughter are precious gifts. We need to treasure them while continually sharing them. They ought to become a priority in our lives.

Humor balances the burdens of life. Sharing laughter with a sad or depressed friend may act as a candle in a dark room. Light, by its very nature, dispels and replaces the darkness.

"Humor balances the burdens of life."

It is important that we surround ourselves with people who make us smile and look on the bright side of life, as well as be that way ourselves. Perhaps we need to watch more young people like Rob and Dan. Research tells us that children laugh, on the average, at least 150 times a day. We should take a lesson from them.

"Courage is not the absence of fear,

but rather the judgment that something

else is more important than fear. "

— *Ambrose Redmoon*

...about courage

My wife, Helen, and I, and our daughter Denise's husband, Gregg, once again found ourselves waiting anxiously in the surgical lounge of a hospital in central Indiana. This was a more regular occurrence than any of us would have wished for. Denise was undergoing her third major surgery in less than four years. Denise's surgeries had all been done to remove cancerous tumors or cancer-related growths that had persisted in spite of previous surgeries and several rounds of chemotherapy.

This particular surgery was to remove a growth which had invaded her spinal cord, causing Denise to lose the use of her legs. She had been using a wheelchair for the past few months. Because of this, she and her husband were selling their condominium and were planning to move into a barrier-free apartment in order to make life a bit easier for her.

She had continued to work in her position as an electronics engineer. In fact while doing so, she had played a major role designing new accommodations to assist others with disabilities at her work site.

As we waited, we knew all too well that such complicated, delicate and extensive surgeries take several hours. Once again, we had waited beyond the expected time for the surgery to be completed. Finally, Dr. Fred came down the hallway and sat with us in one corner of the room. He believed he had removed a significant amount of the tumorous growth that had invaded Denise's spinal cord. However, he felt that there had been a significant amount of damage to the spinal cord, and he was afraid that Denise would never walk again.

Needless to say, this was another devastating blow to all of us. We had heard more than our share of bad news in the past few years, so we felt we were long overdue for something positive. Of course, this was not what Denise was hoping to hear either. She certainly had been through plenty and was looking for some brighter news.

"She certainly had been through plenty and was looking for some brighter news."

A few days later when Denise was discharged from the hospital, she was moved to a new rehabilitation facility. In my many years of working with children with disabilities and their families, I have never visited a hospital or rehabilitation facility like this one. The design was excellent; everything was built with the patients in mind. It was bright and colorful and spacious and had all of the technical equipment necessary for rehabilitation activities. I remember the beautiful grounds at this facility very well. Denise enjoyed the outdoors, and many times I would push her in her wheelchair as we walked around the grounds admiring the trees, flowers, and the occasional small wild animals. We enjoyed this time together.

"…this was simply the beginning of Denise's plan to prove the doctors wrong."

The staff was great also. Denise and one of her therapists developed a very good friendship. There were times, however, when she did not agree with what they told her. A doctor and staff member had told her that she would not walk again, and she had already seen a medical report that had been accidentally left in her room stating the same prognosis. Little did we know that this was simply the beginning of Denise's plan to prove the doctors wrong.

After living in this facility for several weeks and attending regular and frequent therapy sessions, Denise was discharged and returned home to be with Gregg in their apartment. They bought a new bed that could be adjusted electronically to various positions. She continued to do regular exercises at home, and Gregg spent much time and energy assisting her, especially with massage and extensive leg exercises. He was simply fantastic with her. She could not have asked for a better and more helpful husband. We were very proud and happy to have him as a son-in-law.

Over a period of many months, Denise continued to go to therapy on a regular schedule. She rarely missed an appointment. Though we lived a distance away, Helen and I, along with our daughter Sheri and future son-in-law, David, visited whenever we could. On a couple of occasions, Denise asked me to take her to her therapy appointment, and I was happy to do so. I enjoyed the positive atmosphere and the upbeat attitude of the staff. Most of all, I was very impressed with the progress she was making. Of course, the major goal was for her to walk again. I will never forget how proud and thrilled she was to show me how she could stand with her braces on and how she could take small, slow, deliberate steps while holding on to the parallel bars.

The next summer, Sheri was getting married, and Denise was to be the maid of honor in the wedding. A few days before the wedding, Sheri, Denise, and Helen made the customary visit to the dress shop for the formal fitting. While there, Denise stood alone with her braces to see how the dress would look. This was the first time she had stood alone since the surgery. The fitting was temporarily interrupted while the three of them shed tears of joy together for this special event.

"...at the reception, with her braces and Gregg's support, she stood and they danced together."

On Sheri's wedding day, Denise took her place as maid of honor at the ceremony in her wheelchair. Later, at the reception, with her braces and Gregg's support, she stood and they danced together. Many at the reception watched with joy. Most of us will never forget that evening.

In the months ahead, her ability to walk continued to progress. Soon the wheelchair was put into a storage unit near the apartment. Not long after that, the braces were set aside because they were no longer needed. Denise and Gregg were looking for a new home to purchase. It was not long until they told us that they had found a nice ranch on a small lake. We were thrilled for them and helped them move as soon as they closed on the purchase. The dining area as well as the master bedroom looked out over the lake. Their new home provided them the peaceful environment for which they were looking.

> *"She had mustered up the fighting spirit and courage to prove him wrong."*

Several months after her surgery, Denise had occasion to meet again with Dr. Fred. As she sat in his office, he said, "Well, show me what you can do."

She asked him, "What would you like me to do?"

He answered, "Just show me what you 'can' do."

She stood, walked across the room, turned, walked back to her chair, and sat down.

The doctor was quite shocked but very pleased. He did not mind at all that she had mustered up the fighting spirit and courage to prove him wrong.

Denise learned all she could about her cancer, about nutrition, and about various therapy and treatment options.

She was able to walk again, but the cancer continued to take its course. I will never forget one phone message left at our home by her oncologist at the cancer center in Houston, Texas. A reevaluation had been done, and "substantive progression" of tumor growth had been found. It only took me a second to translate that into plain English to mean "the cancer had grown significantly."

As she continued to fight, Denise complained very little and never visibly displayed fear. She was always filled with hope. She was determined and convinced that she would beat her cancer. She apologized for the fact that her illness was causing so much sadness and pain to those around her. In fact, the last time we cried together, I told her how sorry I was to be so helpless on her behalf.

"Much of her spirit, love, courage, and memory live on in this book."

She said, "What bothers me most is not this crazy disease, but how much it is affecting our family and friends."

Denise and Gregg lived in their new home for about two years before she died peacefully there. Much of her spirit, love, courage, and memory live on in this book.

In the dictionary, one definition of courage is "a mental and moral strength enabling one to venture, persevere, and withstand danger, fear, or difficulty firmly and resolutely." As her father, my bias shows, but I believe that describes Denise. She lived it and modeled it for me and for others.

"Life is eternal, and love is immortal, and death is only a horizon; and a horizon is nothing save the limit of our sight."

— Rossiter Worthington Raymond

...about mortality

My grandfather had been resting a bit uneasily. Then he became very still, and his breathing returned to a more normal rhythm. Suddenly his eyes opened wide, and he looked directly at my mother. Then he looked at me and smiled. Less than a minute later, he closed his eyes and took his last breath.

I remember the day very well. It was Easter Sunday, and I was sixteen years old. My mother and I had been to church and were visiting my grandfather. He was being cared for at home because little more could be done for the life-threatening cancer he had been fighting. We were aware that his condition was worsening and that he likely would die soon. We were sad to see him go, but we were glad we had been able to visit him regularly. My grandfather's death was my first experience with death. I have thought about it often and have been thankful that it was a peaceful and a positive experience with death.

Since that Easter Sunday, I have shared in mourning and grieving the deaths of several others. I will never forget visiting my dad in the hospital ICU after he had a heart attack. After talking a bit, he looked at me with tears in his eyes and said, "I am not ready to die." That was the first time I had ever seen him cry. He was right; he was not ready. He lived several more years and was actively involved in landscape work until he died at the age of 78. Though my parents had been divorced and things between my dad and me were sometimes uncomfortable, we talked about a lot of things. It seemed as though we both worked at our relationship, though perhaps unconsciously. I was pleased to feel we had no "unfinished business" when he died.

My mom and I had always had a good relationship, and I watched over her a bit in her later years. She lived in an apartment only a few miles away. Her passing was certainly a sad time, but her health had been deteriorating and she died peacefully at the age of 83. I was glad I could be with her when she died. I continue to be very thankful for all that she did for me and for the many sacrifices she made for my sister and me.

> *"I was pleased to feel we had no 'unfinished business' when he died."*

Years ago, I had a good friend named Tom, whom I never knew when he was healthy. Tom was struggling with an advanced case of emphysema. He had been a heavy smoker for years. When I visited him, he had a difficult time even walking the fifteen steps it took him to get from his

"I still have fond memories of Tom."

bed to the couch in the living room. With assistance, Tom could travel a bit in a car. Most of the time, it was for trips to the doctor.

Tom was a bright man, an excellent electrician who held several special electrical patents. One day at our house, he coached me through the wiring of an entire room while he sat and watched me. Soon after that, Tom was hospitalized, and I visited him several times. I will never forget my last visit with him. By the time I arrived home fifteen minutes later, my wife, Helen, had received a call that Tom had died. Though this was many years ago, I still have fond memories of Tom.

Not long ago, I learned that a good friend with whom I had taught many years ago was struggling with his second bout with cancer. Dick and I had not seen each other in nearly thirty years. I called him to see if I could visit him. He said, "Fine," and sounded pleased that I had called. When I drove into his driveway, he was sitting on his porch. We were both very happy to see each other. We had a great visit and spoke of many mutual friends and coworkers and also about many of the projects we had done together with the students. Though it was great to see Dick, it was obvious that he was in very poor health. He told me he weighed 90 pounds. When I left that afternoon, we hugged and I told him I would return in a couple of weeks for another visit. Dick said, "I am not sure. God has my schedule." He sent me a very kind thank-you note for visiting him. He died a week later.

I have experienced the deaths of numerous other friends, coworkers, and relatives. All these deaths had an effect on me, but nothing could have prepared me for the death of my dear daughter Denise. It brought pain, loss, sadness, and grief for which I have no words to describe. If you have lost a child, you know what I am saying.

Let me share a bit about Denise. She was born on October 13, 1962. Right after I first saw her and Helen, I wrote on a small piece of paper: "The greatness of God is most vividly expressed in the birth of a child to new and loving parents. This alone, through reason, should prove the existence of God to all men." I felt exactly the same way again when our daughter Sheri was born. I still have the original note, still believe it, and find it as relevant to me today as it was then.

My heart sank like nothing I can ever remember the day the doctor reported finding Denise's cancer after completing her initial surgery. Helen and I were both

"Fathers are supposed to fix things for their children, and I could not fix this."

in shock, along with Denise's husband, Gregg. Wandering through the hospital later that morning, I found myself in the chaplain's office. After listening to my story, the chaplain told me that the pain comes from the fact that I am a father and that fathers are supposed to fix things for their children, and I could not fix this. He was right! It was the most helpless feeling in the world. I was the dad but there was nothing I could do to protect my daughter from this dreadful disease that had entered her body. I was not only powerless but afraid. And so my grieving began. We grieve many types of losses, not simply death. The loss of Denise's health was serious. As parents, we certainly would rather endure such an illness ourselves than see one of our children suffer.

Our concern for Denise was returned with her concern for us. She worried more about the effect of her illness on her family and friends than about her own disease. It was obvious that she was trying to care for us and protect us as much as she could throughout her illness.

One time after Denise had undergone extensive surgery at the M. D. Anderson Cancer Center in Houston, I recall asking the doctor, "What would you do if Denise were your daughter?"

He replied softly, "I don't know, but I know I would not give up."

So despite our praying and not giving up, we lost our lovely daughter. Five years after her initial diagnosis, Denise died peacefully in her sleep at her home. I certainly think God took her far too early, but I am thankful to have a part of her still in my heart.

"God took her far too early, but I am thankful to have a part of her still in my heart."

Are we ever given anything we can't handle? I guess not, but we can surely come close. It seemed like we were in a fog for a few months. It was a very difficult time for all of us—for Helen and me, for Denise's husband, and for her younger sister, Sheri, and Sheri's husband, David. My friend Jeff said, "Children being buried by their parents and grandparents is perhaps the hardest of all losses to deal with." Personally, I believe that to be true. A child's death violates all the rules of nature.

At the time of Denise's death, I felt so lonesome. One asks "Why?" It seemed like this tragedy had somehow singled out me and my family, like it was only happening to us. But we knew that was not true. That was made obvious just by reading the local papers for the next two days. Sadly, on the day Denise died, I saw that a bubbly little seven-year-old girl, standing in front of her house, was killed in a drive-by shooting. Also, a father of a two-year-old boy was killed by a reckless driver as he walked to the corner store to pick up some milk. A bright, outgoing sixteen-year-old girl was shot and killed by her boyfriend. A little six-year-old boy died after a four year battle with cancer. I knew I was not alone that day; it just seemed that way. We all are faced with adversity, tragedy, and death. The important thing is to find the necessary strength, support, and faith to weather the storm.

When Denise died, I wondered if I could ever be happy again. I journeyed through the shock, anger, sadness, disbelief, fear, and even depression. Might a broken heart be a better description than depression? Everyone has his own unique way of dealing with loss and grief. If I were to be happy and enjoy myself, would I be untrue to Denise? I know now that it was not a question of whether I will ever be happy again, but a question of whether I will ever be the same again. The answer to that is no. But life goes on, and I do still have many things for which to be happy and thankful. Life does pretty much return to normal, but it is a "new" kind of normal because of the experience. A piece of my heart seems to be missing, and an important piece of my life is gone. I will cherish the memories I have of my daughter's laughter and her thoughtfulness, wisdom, and love. I can still picture Denise and Sheri riding on their beautiful Morgan horses. Those and many other memories will never leave me. Just because she is out of my sight, she has not been removed from my heart. Part of her will always be with me.

"I cherish the memories I have of my daughter's laughter and her thoughtfulness, wisdom, and love."

Yes, it is true we never really get over a loss like this. But we do find ways to move on in our lives, and we must. Our loved ones always wanted the best for us while they were here with us. Why would they wish anything different for us now that they are gone? Denise would not want me to mope and continue to grieve. In fact, I believe she would be quite upset with me if that were the path I had chosen. Instead, she would want me to be positive and spend my energy helping others and doing some good.

"She would want me to be positive and spend my energy helping others and doing some good."

In recent years, I have worked as a hospice volunteer. My work in this area has been most rewarding as well as humbling. I enjoy a fine relationship with the great hospice staff and other volunteers. I have also gained valuable training and have formed special relationships with many patients and their families.

In my hospice work, once again, the feeling of helplessness is so evident. Illness is beyond our control, especially serious terminal illness. Chaos often enters the life of the patient and his or her loved ones. Terminal illness often involves much hard work; it can be exhausting and consuming. The dying person has many needs that must be met by the caregiver or by other relatives, friends, and professionals.

Support from all who care is a treasure to the patient and to their loved ones at a very difficult time. A hospice volunteer can help a patient live his last days a bit more comfortably and with a bit more dignity, and I believe the patient feels less isolated and alone. Loved ones and families cannot be with the patient at all times, and I have found families to be tremendously gracious and appreciative of the services of hospice volunteers. There really is nothing painful or frightening about sitting with a dying patient and holding his or her hand. It is not alarming to watch the peaceful death of a human being when one knows everything has been done to help and the time to leave has come. We don't know our hospice patients very long, but they do touch our lives. I believe those I have had the honor of visiting have left me stronger and a bit wiser.

About 80% of the deaths in our country take place in nursing homes or in hospitals, even though most people would prefer to die in the comfortable surroundings of their own home. The ill and dying need people and companionship. Often they are lonely and sad, and often they die alone.

We are fortunate if we are able to be close by or with them when they die. At the same time, we must not feel guilty if we are not able to be present at the time of a loved one's death. Many times, people choose to die when they feel they will cause the least commotion. I have read countless examples where people have died alone in the early morning hours. They have spared their loved ones the pain of witnessing their death. It is not always possible to do everything we believe would have been appropriate. I believe that we all do the very best we can at the time and under the circumstances.

"It may seem as though the dying are waiting for our permission to leave."

Concern for loved ones is often shared by the dying individual. We need to listen carefully to their messages. They may be preparing us by talking about traveling, packing, or taking a trip. They want to be reassured that the loved ones they leave behind will be okay. Sometimes it may seem as though the dying are waiting for our permission to leave. They may need our assurance that all is okay and we will be alright. Sharing from the heart at times like this can be helpful to both parties and can leave good memories.

It is important for people who are dying to feel like they have contributed something worthwhile and influenced others in a positive way while they were here. Recently, I spoke with a man who has cancer. Two years ago, he was given one year to live. He expects to die soon and is not afraid. He does, however, want to find a way to be an inspiration to his many children, several of whom are adopted.

Our lives are touched in so many ways by those we love and care about. We continue to be influenced by them even after we have placed their bodies in the ground.

We will never be the same after the death of a loved one. Healing takes time. Our pain, guilt, anger, sorrow, and grief are all natural. They are the path to our healing. We must allow ourselves to grieve and not hold it in. Each of us experiences loss and grief differently. We must be patient with ourselves and others. For others, the pain is often as deep as our own. We can be a great help by encouraging and supporting others who are also hurting.

> *"Our lives are touched in so many ways by those we love and care about."*

Grief comes in waves. We should not hide from our pain when it comes. We may simply need to let it stay for a while, then pick ourselves up and go on until the next wave comes. Closure may not come soon. Time is not a measure of our healing. We will heal at our own unique pace. We must remember that there is nothing wrong with our personal process of grieving. It is certainly not a sign of weakness. Tears and mourning are natural and are necessary if we are going to heal. Like a broken bone, we need attention and time to mend. But once healed, that bone is stronger in the broken places. I am confident that our hearts will be too.

—⊱◈⊰—

Certainly, as each of us gets on with age, we will have more occasions to witness death. A friend of mine asked recently, "Should death really be so unexpected?" It is, after all, a predetermined event established at the time of conception. We enter this life and we leave it. Death is as much a part of life as is birth, but death is certainly a much more difficult topic to deal with.

Not long ago, a friend shared with me that she and her husband were nearly ready to retire, as were their good friends Mary and Al. The four of them had spent a lot of time together and were looking forward to spending much of their retirement doing the same. "Mary died last week," my friend said. "She ruined all of our plans." My friend loved Mary as a sister and was not being disrespectful, but she meant what she said.

This life of ours does not rewind. It is not fair. Perhaps we should stop expecting it to be. It seems that adversity and heartbreak are not distributed evenly. However, we do all get a share. At times in our lives, our plates get pretty full. Each of our lives is filled with different "stuff." If we really knew the truth, it may be very hard for us to envy anyone. None of us has been given any guarantees that our lives will be free of pain, disappointment, or tragedy.

"This life of ours does not rewind."

We have every right to be upset when things happen that seem unfair, especially when we experience the death of a loved one. Often it is hard to find peace of mind. We feel empty and tired. We miss holding their face close to ours and holding them in our arms. We realize that our daily affairs and our earthly possessions matter little compared to our relationships with those whom we love. The memories we have will be far more durable than the things we accumulate. I would wager that if each of us had only thirty minutes to live, every cell phone and telephone line on the planet would be in use. I remember a cartoon in which a little boy wanted some attention from his mom and dad. He said, "Your housework and paper will always be here. I won't." What a great message!

My friends who are cancer survivors or have had other brushes with death exhibit an obvious appreciation for life. They seem to enjoy each day that is given them. For them, the sky seems bluer, the clouds whiter, the grass greener, and the colorful flowers more fragrant. We can learn from them.

"By removing the clutter from our lives, we will be able to see more clearly what is really important."

Our energy should be directed toward living life to its fullest. The contributions you and I make in this lifetime are not measured by how long we are here or by the number of breaths we take. Rather, they are measured by what we have done and by what we have given. By removing the clutter from our lives, we will be able to see more clearly what is really important.

If we have lived a full life, we will be pleased when we look back on it. We will not feel that our time has been wasted.

We welcome the joyous times when things go well, but these times do not help us to grow. It is the times of adversity that stretch our limits and change us. We must accept the fact that we will have difficult times in this life. As one pastor explained to me, "After all, we know that Christ endured pain and suffering while on earth." I don't believe that God causes pain and suffering, but He allows it because of sin in our world. Yet, we are not asked to endure these hardships alone. We have each other to lean on for help, and we have our spiritual resources from which we can draw strength. My spirituality inspires my personal philosophy of life and death. I know this life of loss and sorrow will not last forever. My hope is greatly reinforced by my belief that I will be reunited with Denise and other loved ones at a future time. That brings me peace.

We all have tucked the fond memories of our loved ones away inside our hearts. A living memorial to them might be our acts of compassion toward others. That may not only help our healing, but it will multiply the good in this imperfect world of ours.

Let us see life more clearly and realize that each breath is precious in this circle of life. We can remember with love those we have lost, and at the same time, welcome with joy the excitement we see in a new mother's eyes. Tomorrow, we may hold the hand of a dying loved one, or we may hold a new born baby with the same gentleness.

You and I only get to live life one time, but if we do it well, once is enough. We understand that sunshine always returns after the dark clouds and rain, and with it comes the possibility and promise of a beautiful rainbow.

"I shall pass through this world but once. Any good thing therefore that I can do, or any kindness that I can show to any human being, let me do it now. Let me not defer it or neglect it, for I shall not pass this way again."

— *Etienne de Grellet*

...about support

It was around 6:00 AM on a cold November morning. As I sat on the sofa, crying and in shock, I felt a hand grip my shoulder. The grip was firm and caring. It brought a steady, comforting stability to my otherwise chaotic being. My wife, Helen, and I were in central Indiana at the home of our daughter Denise and her husband, Gregg. Denise had passed away earlier that morning. Though she had courageously battled cancer for the last five years, her death was still unexpected.

I was about to make the most difficult phone call of my life; I was calling our younger daughter, Sheri, to tell her that her sister had died. I was barely able to speak. Through the entire phone call, I was aware of the strong hand on my shoulder. After I hung up the phone, I turned and saw a priest standing behind the sofa. His hand was still on my shoulder. He obviously knew what I was going through. I do not know who he was or who had called him, but I thanked him for being there for us.

He stayed awhile and then left. I have not seen him since.

What he did may not seem like much, yet that small gesture of support was the best thing he could have done for me at the time. The memory of those few moments will remain with me for the rest of my life.

"You don't have to do anything extraordinary to make a difference."

I could have shared other stories of support instead of this one, but I chose this story because it shows how a very simple action can have a truly significant effect. You don't have to do anything extraordinary to make a difference.

Unfortunately, people often hesitate to come forward during difficult times because they don't know what to do or say. They find avoidance a more comfortable choice. How regrettable this is at a time when people who are ill or are suffering a loss need support the most.

A few years ago, some cancer patients offered several suggestions regarding ways in which their friends could be more helpful. These suggestions can apply to anyone suffering a loss or illness.

Their first suggestion was just to "say or do something." The risk of hurting others by saying the wrong thing is less than the risk of hurting them through silence. Saying nothing can be perceived as not caring. If you have difficulty with words, you can "Say it with flowers," or food, or a card. If you can't get beyond this symbolic form of help, then continue to repeat it throughout their time of illness or distress.

When making conversation, don't avoid the uncomfortable subject of their illness or possible death but confront it directly. Tell them you're sorry to learn about their situation. That gives

"Tears from a friend are comforting to someone in distress. It shows that you care."

them the choice to either talk about or not talk about it. If they choose to talk about it, be a good listener. Share your own feelings also. Tears from a friend are comforting to someone in distress. It shows that you care. If they change the subject, it doesn't mean you have said the wrong thing. You've let them know that you are willing to share difficult feelings with them, so they may bring it up later when they feel like talking about it.

The cancer patients also reflected on what is not helpful.

Do not advise them on how to bear up under their adversity. Also, if their situation is not correctable, don't try to make things better by offering false cheer. They don't expect you to fix their situation. They mostly want you to be willing to share the bad news.

Don't make generalized offers to help by telling them to call if there's anything you can do. Make specific offers and don't stop offering, even if they've told you no. It is difficult for many people to accept help from others, and they may need a little push. Wait a few days and offer again.

These are only suggestions, but they may help us all feel more comfortable when approaching a friend who is experiencing difficult circumstances. Don't let awkwardness keep you away. It is difficult for anyone to fight an illness, and one certainly does not want to do it alone. People who are ill may want to talk, joke around, and be able to feel as normal as possible. They may still be interested in things at work or current events. A sick person still has feelings, dreams, and opinions they want to share.

Though communication may be uncomfortable at times, it can result in honest, open sharing. The person facing difficulties may need a chance to release anger and fear. It may be necessary to discuss and resolve areas of unfinished business. Talking honestly can often bring peace rather than discomfort. Increased understanding and closeness are very important at a time like this. When we listen and share our hearts, we are showing our love and concern.

Support not only is needed for those who are ill, but it is also necessary for the people who are close to a person who is ill or has died. They are hurting too. A friend sent a note to me after Denise died. "I hear so many people say that they do not know what to say to you. I have to be honest. I don't know what to say either. I want so much to say the right thing to ease the pain you feel, but I can't."

"When we listen and share our hearts, we are showing our love and concern."

A relative wrote, "I had hoped to find words that could somehow comfort you at this difficult time, but..." I understood their messages very well. They tried. They cared. They wrote. It helped a lot. We all remember people we knew who were ill, and we were at a loss for the "right words" to say. Is that not often the case at funeral homes? We may find it easier for tears to come to our eyes than for words to come to our mouths. Even though our words may seem inadequate, the important thing is that we are present and we try.

Your friends and loved ones need to know that in spite of all the changes in their lives, your friendship is one thing that will not change. The burdens of life are lighter when they are shared.

⎯⎯◆⎯⎯

We live in a world full of hurting people. They need us to hold them, hug them, and cry with them. Quite often, they simply need us to listen. Each of us wants to feel cared about, especially in times of stress and difficulty. This is as true for a child who has had a negative incident at school or has lost a pet, as it is for a friend at the funeral home who has just lost a loved one. We have daily opportunities to provide support to others. Even the smallest gesture, like the grip of a caring hand, may have lasting effects. A little bit of love and support goes a long way.

"Whatever you can do, or dream you can do, begin it. Boldness has genius, power and magic in it."

— *Goethe*

…about adoption

On a mild winter evening in January, my wife and I arrived at the local airport and joined others to wait at Gate #1 for passengers to disembark from an incoming flight. We had not seen the plane land, but it was close to being on schedule. About forty friends and relatives of our daughter Sheri and son-in-law David had gathered in the roped off area. We waited attentively as the passengers from the plane filed through the gate. Many of the passengers greeted people waiting for them, while others went directly to the baggage claim area. Then the line stopped, but the people we were waiting for had not yet left the plane.

Then as I glanced at Gate #1, I saw a little boy wearing a white shirt and bib overalls. He was such a little guy, not two years old yet. He took a few short, slow steps out from the gate into the room where we waited. This little person was our new grandson, Dima, and his new mom and dad were only a few steps behind him. He had just traveled half-way around the world to his new home. He was taking his first steps into his totally new world and new life. No doubt, seeing all the people there to meet him and his mom and dad was a bit overwhelming. But needless to say, we were thrilled to see all three of them arrive safely. Sheri and David had just completed a trip around the world to bring Dima home.

In December of that same year, Sheri and David made another similar trip to bring Nadya, Dima's older sister, and Alex, his older brother, to their new home. Again, a large group welcomed these little ones to their new home and new life. My wife, Helen, and I now had three wonderful new grandchildren. Little did we know at the times of their arrival how much excitement, pleasure, joy, and love they would bring into our lives.

"Little did we know at the times of their arrival how much excitement, pleasure, joy, and love they would bring into our lives."

These three little people had been born in far eastern Russia and had been living in an orphanage in the beautiful region of Kamchatka.

Quite often parents choose international adoption because they have heard many horror stories regarding domestic adoptions. One fear is that the birth mother may later change her mind, and the new parents may then lose the child. Domestic adoptions, however, are usually far less complicated and happen in a much shorter time period; I am told that many can be completed in a few weeks. International adoptions are usually much more involved. With our grandchildren, the entire process, from beginning to end, took nearly 2 1/2 years. My daughter Sheri has often likened the international adoption process to a roller coaster ride. There are certainly many ups and downs before you finally reach your destination and final goal where the adoption is complete.

"There are certainly many ups and downs before you finally reach your destination and final goal, where the adoption is complete."

Several adoption agencies work with families seeking to adopt from other countries. Approximately 100 Chinese children are adopted by American families each week, and Russian adoption numbers are not far behind. In many cases, countries like Russia require that the couple visit the child and the orphanage before they can bring the child home. In some cases, as with our grandchildren, it may require two trips. Other countries handle all of the paperwork and financial matters through the agency, and the children are "delivered" to the new parents. The realities of international adoptions are many, but it is clear to me that persistence and determination are necessary to successfully complete an international adoption.

> *"Persistence and determination are necessary to successfully complete an international adoption."*

The instability of foreign governments plays an important role in whether adoptions are "open" to foreigners. In Rumania, Russia, China and other countries, adoptions may close abruptly for no apparent reason. When a foreign government closes adoptions temporarily, many excited but frustrated parents must place their plans on hold. The rules of course come from the bureaucracy. Often, adoptive parents are frustrated by what seem to be unrealistic and unnecessary expectations. Adoptions may take two to three times as long as a pregnancy. A change of rules in midstream may force prospective parents to start over, not only with paperwork, but also with fingerprints, home studies, and so on.

Many ask, "Why must it be so hard and costly?" There are legal fees, agency fees, and of course, gifts to buy. Clothes must be bought for your new child, for everything he or she wears at the orphanage must be left there. There are piles of papers to fill out, home studies to prepare for, passports and visas to obtain, and then more paperwork. What about travel, lodging, food, and non-contaminated water? Medical reports on the adoptive parents must be sent. But don't forget the shots. Did you remember to send the bank statements? And you must send the photo album with the pictures of your home and family, including the dog, to the director of the orphanage. Oh yes, there are the interviews, state police checks, letters of reference, the marriage license, birth certificates, the Immigration and Naturalization Service, and more paperwork. In many cases, the time line for adoption only begins when the paperwork is totally completed. Of course, that process also includes many items being notarized and often translated. Delays are almost a normal part of the process; sometimes adoptions are held up for months. If the parents of the children are still alive, the children must be declared orphans, and the birth parents must sign off. Only then can the child be placed on the registry. In Russia, for example, the child must then remain on the registry for three months before becoming eligible for adoption.

Staff at the orphanages are not anxious to let children go with American families and other foreigners. There is a hope among the Russian people and the orphanage staff that a Russian family will adopt them first. For the most part, that is simply wishful thinking and occurs rarely.

Try to imagine that you are going to adopt a child from Russia. You dream about how wonderful it would be to have one of these children in your home and in your life. First, you are sent videos, medical reports, and photographs of one or more children that are available for adoption; they're adorable, and within the age ranges requested. You are told to study the information and go with your gut feelings. And so you fall in love with a referral, with a photo of a child you are sent. You are ready to make a commitment only to find that the same photo and information have been sent to several other couples. This child cannot become yours because another family spoke up first and is adopting her. You wonder, "How can they do this? Why would they offer the same child to several families?"

> *"You dream about how wonderful it would be to have one of these children in your home and in your life."*

You realize so many factors are outside of your control. You become angry and upset, and rightly so. Will you persist or quit? It is complicated, time-consuming, and very stressful. Now you understand why so many people give up. Adoption agency coordinators and staff remind you that persistent families are successful in their attempt to adopt. As one said, "For them giving up is not an option." You remember that nothing worthwhile is easy.

"Remember that nothing worthwhile is easy."

So you start over. You consider another child. He has been offered only to you and will not be offered to others unless you decide not to take him. But you want him! So you move ahead. You tell the agency, and the wheels start moving. You are told, "Be ready to travel at a moment's notice." You hope all the paperwork is being completed properly and the necessary approvals are secured.

If you have other children at home, you make plans for their care while you are gone. You will have enough to do without having to concern yourself with their care and safety. You prepare for the trip, hoping you won't find that election results have changed adoption availability. You have heard stories about lost paperwork, inexperienced adoption or orphanage staff, and even offices being moved or closed.

You make the necessary payments and prepare to take extra cash with you. You know that before you are done, the adoption of one child will cost you a minimum of ten thousand dollars. You wonder sometimes where all the money goes. You are told to bring "new" cash since there is a concern about counterfeit money. The bills are often put through a scanner. Many things are paid for personally in cash.

> *"The adoption of one child will cost you a minimum of ten thousand dollars."*

You work hard to find out what the roles of the adoption coordinators are, both at your agency and at the site of the orphanage. Will she interpret? Will she check to see that all the paperwork is completed properly? Will she get all the necessary approvals from the proper authorities? Will she be able to have documents notarized when needed? Will she fly at least part of the way home with you and your new son, since you cannot speak each other's language?

Finally, you are on your way. You travel to the Moscow airport and find dark hallways and Aeroflot planes that look like they may not be your first choice for your next flight. You later discover that with resources limited, the Russians have wisely chosen to use the money for maintenance and repair rather than the outward appearance of the plane. Sheri and David told me that their flight across Russia on Aeroflot was one of the best they'd had on their first trip around the world.

You arrive in Moscow and realize that you will need to make some adjustments. A healthy approach to visiting would be "expect the unexpected" and "go with the flow." Your adoption coordinators are very helpful, for they know the problems people encounter and the questions they ask. For example, public toilets usually have no toilet seat and rarely

> *"A healthy approach to visiting would be 'expect the unexpected' and 'go with the flow.'"*

have toilet paper; you simply take your own paper. Another option might be to use a "pay" public toilet, and then at least some paper would be provided.

Offices that you may need to deal with may not make change or accept credit cards. Though more merchandise is now available since the downfall of the Soviet Union, shopping is still often a time consuming experience. Many stores have only one cashier to handle money from all the purchases in the store. As in any large, unfamiliar city, you will want to be prudent and careful. At the same time, with the proper company or guide, you should certainly try to see such things as St. Basil's, Red Square, the Kremlin, and other historic sites.

> *"The vast majority of orphanage staff members are dedicated, understanding, hard-working, and compassionate."*

On your adoption journey, you must go to the Ministry of Education to obtain permission to visit the orphanages. Adequate hotel facilities are often available within a short distance of the orphanages. Meals out with your adoption coordinator or orphanage director are most often paid by you, the adopting family. A child care worker earns about $20.00 a month in Russia. From what I have read and been told by Sheri, the vast majority of orphanage staff members are dedicated, understanding, hard-working, and compassionate people. There simply are not enough of them.

At the orphanage, some children may come running to you saying "mama" or "papa." They all know that these strangers are probably there to pick up a child. Their eyes stay on you. "Why not me?" they seem to be asking.

Some things appear to be a bit unusual. The children have no experience drinking from a bottle. Many of them do not talk at fifteen months. It is not unusual for many children in orphanages to rock themselves to sleep. They are not allowed to have pacifiers or to suck their thumbs, and the orphanages certainly do not have enough staff to rock the children. The staff select the children's food, and they would like you to feed the child the same food after you take him. "But, what is it?" you ask. You don't recognize that "mush." The available water must be boiled to destroy the parasites if it is to be used for drinking or cooking or mixing with powdered milk. You notice that some of the children have physical problems; in fact, a few may have a deformity of some sort. Others may exhibit behavioral problems or simply appear to be overactive. In some cases, there is little information about the child. Birth parents may even be unknown. Results from health tests may not be reliable. In Russia, tuberculosis and polio are still far more common than in the U.S. You are asked to not hold the orphanage and the doctors responsible.

Now you have met "your" child and are getting to know him. You spend several hours each day with him. Only a few more days and a few more hoops to jump through, and you are on your way to America with him.

You pray that nothing more goes wrong or causes delays: no more missing signatures, closed offices, added paperwork, or changed court dates. Should these problems cause delays, visas may expire. That would cause financial penalties and flight changes which would be difficult to make. You hope all goes smoothly.

You leave the orphanage for the last time today with your son. This is more emotional than you thought it would be.

"Staff members cry as the child leaves, hugging him and making the sign of the cross on his forehead."

Your son says good-bye to his friends and to the staff. Staff members cry as the child leaves, hugging him and making the sign of the cross on his forehead. They also make the sign on your foreheads, as the new parents. As you walk out with your son, the other children watch and wonder. Might it be their turn next time?

As you leave, you think about all the emotions and all the changes that you have been dealing with. You think about the future and make plans in your mind. What about this boy? He is a little human life with feelings and emotions also. He is leaving a familiar structure with many friends and a staff who loves him. Now he is going with two adult strangers into a life of unknowns, and he can't even talk to them. Why wouldn't he feel insecure? His real mother gave him up to an orphanage, which then became his security and his "mother." Now he learns that this, too, was only temporary, and he is being given up again. Can he trust that this next home and these new parents will be for real? What will happen now?

"Can he trust that his next home and these new parents will be for real?"

Your new son has remained at the orphanage since he arrived there. Now he sees cars, buses, trains, and boats. As he rides with you, his face shows fear and amazement. Your flight from the orphanage to Moscow is very long and takes several hours. Your next stop is the American Medical Center in Moscow, where your child will be checked one last time by a doctor. The last stop before you are able to leave the country is the U.S. Embassy. You still need to get your visas and passports before your flight tomorrow. You hope there are no more problems. Did the parents sign the necessary release so you can get your son's visa? You wait in a large room with many other couples with children, knowing full well that each of them has their own unique adoption story.

Your next test is the long flight home. You have learned to communicate, mostly by signs. You still cannot speak to each other in anything resembling real language. You and your son are going through major adjustments. On your trip and in your home, your son learns that food will not be scarce, toys will not be taken from him, and human touch is frequent. Many of us take our homes for granted, but your new son is just learning the true meaning, purpose, and value of "home." Together, through tensions, tears, and joy, you grow to be a family.

"Through tensions, tears, and joy, you grow to be a family."

Your son was one of the thousands of wonderful children waiting to be adopted. He is very lucky, and so are you. He is learning rapidly about the important place he holds in your lives.

The adoption story of my grandchildren is very close to my heart. It carries with it a powerful message of persistence, compassion, and love.

As you know, the adoption process can be involved and trying. I know that we would not have three new grandchildren to enjoy had Sheri and David not chosen to persist. One of Sheri's friends told her that they brought a whole new meaning to "labor and delivery." They would not accept anything less than the successful adoption of these three children, who are now all U.S. citizens. Nadya, Alex, and Dima now belong to a loving "forever" family.

Thousands of foreign children are adopted into American homes each year. U.S. families adopt more of these children than families in all other countries combined. But for every child who is adopted, hundreds more are left behind. Today, nearly one million orphans live in Russian orphanages. The older children have very little chance of being adopted. Children are put onto the streets of Russia between the ages of fourteen and sixteen. Girls may be subjected to abuse, molestation, or even rape. Their future may well include prostitution. Boys may end up in prison, the Mafia, or dead.

Many friends comment about how lucky my grandchildren are to be adopted by a fine young couple who is willing to love and care for them. This is true, and their parents are also lucky to have these neat kids. They are a special gift to us, as grandparents also. Four years before their adoption, our family suffered the tragic loss of Sheri's older sister, Denise. These three new family members have brought our family new light and life. I could never have imagined how much happiness, fun, and love they would have brought us. We are all blessed.

> *"These three new family members have brought our family new light and life."*

Our world is filled with hurting people. For many, there is little we can do, but for these young children, we can bring help. You can change the life of a child and bring a great deal of joy to your own life. You don't need to be an important or famous person to be a loving, adoptive parent, but you can be a hero to one of these precious children. One may be waiting just for you.

"Nobody can do for little children what grandparents do. Grandparents sort of sprinkle stardust over the lives of little children."

— *Alex Haley*

...about grandchildren

I had just arrived at the home of my grandchildren, Nadya, Alex, and Dima. Thirty seconds after I opened the front door, I felt a little person clinging to my leg. Looking down, I saw sparkling little eyes and a big smile that sent the message, "Good morning, Grandpa. I am glad that you are here." My three-year-old grandson, Dima, had come downstairs to greet me. I can think of nothing that would warm my heart more than an early morning greeting and smile from one of my three special grandchildren.

A few years ago, my wife, Helen, and I chose to take on the regular responsibility of caring for our three young grandchildren during their preschool years while their parents were at work. We loved it. It was actually the best job I have ever had. Now that they're older, we still provide care periodically and remain actively involved with them.

I have enjoyed many great experiences with my grandchildren. Of the many fun times we've shared, I must say that our sleep-over camp-outs bring some of the fondest memories. I still don't quite understand how "Grandpa" is always chosen to be the one to sleep in the tent with the kids. I think their mom, dad, and grandma must have some special voting process going on. But I probably would feel slighted if I didn't get to enjoy this fun opportunity to be with my grandchildren, even if the ground isn't as soft as my bed.

Their mother has said that it takes the three of them a long time to pack for these camping trips. Actually, they are not the kind of trips that take a great deal of planning or special equipment and supplies. In fact, the "wilderness" is Grandma and Grandpa's backyard, and the tent is set up about forty feet from our back door. Not only is the tent near our house, the porch light is left on, and grandma sleeps on a couch close to the unlocked door. If anyone needs to use the bathroom, they go inside the house. It's really roughing it!

> *"The fun begins when we set up the tent."*

The fun begins when we set up the tent. At first, we used a smaller tent, but recently, I bought a larger, nicer one.

The children are expected to help put it up and get their blankets and sleeping bags ready for the night. They don't really mind. Nadya admitted, "It takes a long time to set up the tent, but I don't care because I get to sleep in it. It's warm and cuddly with all the blankets." Dima said, "It looks cool inside. We have a lot of fun playing there."

I asked the children to share some of their memories of our camping events. Of course, they remembered the bugs. We would always get a few mosquito bites, even with insect repellent and the screens zipped shut. Dima reminded me about all the ants, and Alex didn't forget the big, black bug. He recalled, "It took Grandpa a long time to get it out of the tent." Nadya remembered hearing all the crickets in the night. It's hard to believe, but she also remembered hearing Grandpa snore.

"He was brave enough to stay and keep Grandpa company."

Alex recalled that one night both Nadya and Dima went into the house and stayed there for the rest of the night. He bragged, "I was still in the tent with Grandpa." He thought it was great that he was brave enough to stay and keep Grandpa company.

One thing that all three of the children remembered well was that I would read mystery stories to them. We would all snuggle up in our sleeping bags, and using my flashlight, I would read *Moon Beach Mysteries.* After the stories, we would talk a bit and then try to get some sleep.

One morning, I remember waking up and looking around the tent and noticing, to my surprise, that I was all alone. There were three empty sleeping bags but no children. They had all gone into the house, each for a different reason. Dima told me he had gotten cold. Alex said he saw some bugs he didn't like. And I had to chuckle when Nadya said, "I woke up and those birds kept singing so loud that I couldn't go back to sleep." But on most camping nights, the kids stuck it out with their dear old grandpa, and we had a great time. I know this isn't the last of our camping excursions, and I am sure the children and I will always remember these fun times.

Spending time with my grandchildren is an important priority for me. It has once again reacquainted me with the wonderful world of little people. I need to remind myself that they are, in fact, children and not small adults. They are on a journey to become big people; it's a journey we must allow them to enjoy and take slowly. We should help them celebrate who they are today, their age, and their individuality. Children manage to teach us the importance of living and enjoying life now.

Nadya, Alex, and Dima are full of imagination and creativity, as are most children. Their energy and enthusiasm are contagious. Being with them has helped to keep me young physically, as well as young at heart. They can spend hours playing together and pretending. From their dress-up area, they use dresses, hats, boots, and glasses, only to mention a few. They then act out such roles as moms, dads, firemen, cowboys, doctors, as well as cooks and many others. You can imagine some of the meals they have made for

> *"Children manage to teach us the importance of living and enjoying life now."*

me. Their creativity is also evident in their artwork. Sometimes it's hard to find the refrigerator under all the pictures, notes, and cards they have made for us.

Children's young minds are eager to soak up information, and my grandchildren are no exception. They continually challenge me with their questions. Try answering one of these: "Why is God invisible?" Nadya asked. Alex wanted to know, "How do they get the deer to cross the road where they put those signs?" And Dima once asked, "Grandpa, will you still be alive when I get growed up?" This one caused me to ponder the most. But it also made me realize the importance of talking about such things. Children will lose their grandparents. Obviously, Dima had thought about it. When they inquire, it may be helpful to talk to them about life cycles and the natural course of life and death. If they have lost a pet, that could be used as an example. Then let them express their thoughts and feelings.

As parents and grandparents, we can help children understand the importance of generations and families. Children need to realize that they are a valuable part of their family and they will always be accepted in that family. This gives them a sense of belonging. They need to know they are loved. When we love them unconditionally, they feel comfortable and safe. The approval of parents and grandparents is very important. They try so hard to please us. We should encourage and support them. It's important to praise them for the specific things they have done well, but we also need to assure them

"Grandpa, will you still be alive when I get growed up?"

that their self-worth is not based upon their achievements, grades, or success. We will love them no matter what.

When Helen and I care for our grandchildren, we try to help them make wise choices and take responsibility for the choices they have made. At the same time, we realize they must be given opportunities to make mistakes. We hope they will be minor ones, such as skinning a knee, rather then breaking a leg. We do our best to teach them safety. They must be prepared to accept difficult moments and learn how to deal with them. Helen is especially good at helping the children solve problems on their own.

Now that I have spent a significant amount of time with my grandchildren, I sometimes reflect on when our own children, Denise and Sheri, were young. I wonder if I had the same appreciation for them when they were growing up. They certainly were a priority, but as young adults, we were busy with our careers, graduate schools, and special projects. Now that I am a retired grandpa and I am not immersed in work, I want to make good use of my time. That includes spending time with my grandchildren. I admire their parents who are able to handle many responsibilities at work and at home and at the same time, enjoy every minute of the children growing up.

I probably could be accused of being more permissive as a grandparent. Aren't most grandparents guilty of that? I might also be a bit more relaxed, tolerant, and patient. I try to take time to listen. We grandparents have a different perspective of life. I believe we are wiser than we used to be when it comes to developing new relationships. I hope I am more capable of enhancing the lives of those I love, especially the lives of my grandchildren.

———✦———

As grandparents, Helen and I feel very fortunate to be close to our grandchildren and to have the opportunity to watch them grow. They have been a delight to us. It must be difficult when grandparents are not able to see their grandchildren often, for whatever reason. Distance often is a factor, but fortunately with today's technology, there are numerous ways in which grandparents and grandchildren can still keep close ties, even when they do not live nearby.

Long-distance grandparents might consider one of the following ways of enhancing their relationships with their grandchildren. They can make phone calls specifically to their grandchildren and have notes of special things to talk about, such as school activities, friends, hobbies, pets, and so forth. Their grandchildren may enjoy reading something to them over the phone, especially if they are just learning, or they may want to sing a new song, or play one for them on a musical instrument. Pictures also help to keep families close. Today, pictures can be sent by mail or e-mail or fax. Videos are even better, and grandchildren can send back videos or pictures in return. Audiotapes are also fun to receive. E-mail is another wonderful way to keep in touch, and cards and letters will never be obsolete. You don't have to wait for special occasions. Everyone loves getting personal mail.

Some of these things may not be available to all grandparents, but any one of them will be important for their grandchildren to have in years to come. Such things will help them recall fond

"You don't have to wait for special occasions. Everyone loves getting personal mail."

memories of their grandparents. No doubt, it takes extra effort, but special relationships can exist when grandparents and grandchildren are miles apart. And who knows what other wonderful communication advances might occur in the future.

On the other end of the spectrum, many grandparents today are raising or adopting their grandchildren because of various events and circumstances in their families. These special people deserve credit and admiration.

Whether grandparents and grandchildren communicate from afar or spend time together close by, they can learn about each other and develop a loving relationship. This is the thread that connects one generation to the next. Even if the relationship is only for a few years, the time should be cherished and spent wisely.

"Grandchildren see way beyond the wrinkles in our skin."

Grandchildren see way beyond the wrinkles in our skin. They see the special people we are in their lives. They appreciate our love and sacrifices and show their appreciation with hugs and "thank-yous." We hold a significant place in their hearts, and they in ours. No matter how these special little ones come to us, they are a blessing.

I still have many things I would like to do with my grandchildren. I hope they will join me in delivering gifts to orphanages, volunteering in soup kitchens, and visiting my very special hospice patients. I'd like them to become aware of some of the more serious aspects in life and hopefully instill in them a desire to help.

But on the lighter side, someday I plan to corral the three of them into the back yard on a warm summer day. We'll lie on our backs in the grass and study the fluffy white clouds overhead.

"Hey, that one looks like a dog."

"Over there's a chicken."

"Look, I can see a dinosaur."

It's great fun reliving my childhood with my grandchildren. Life doesn't get any better than this!

“*The weak can never forgive.*

Forgiveness is the attribute

of the strong. **”**

— *Mahatma Gandhi*

...about forgiveness

Christmas music was still playing softly as I looked out the window. Two inches of snow had fallen, and it was still coming down. About a dozen of us lingered at the end of our annual office Christmas get-together late on a mid-December afternoon. A small group of staff members had planned the event, which included a few fun games, skits, and delicious refreshments. The tables throughout the room sported bright coverings and modest, but attractive, decorations. The event, though nothing elaborate, had again proven to be a success. It brought the staff together in a more relaxed setting and provided an atmosphere that contributed to the holiday spirit.

I was walking over to fill my coffee cup when I saw Angie sitting alone at a table. Roger and Lois had been sitting with her, but they were now on their way out the door. Angie was an early childhood teacher whom I had recommended for employment in our district nearly ten years earlier. She was an excellent teacher.

Since I had not seen Angie for a while, I joined her at her table. After a minute or two of the usual greetings and shop talk, we spoke a bit about our plans for the holidays and the Christmas break, which school employees look forward to as much as the children.

After we had spoken for a few minutes, Angie said, "You know, I enjoy Christmas mainly because I have three children and a husband, but there is one part of the holidays that I just hate. I get so angry and frustrated because it almost ruins the whole thing for our family and for many others as well."

I said, "Wow, it sounds like something major."

Angie replied, "You're right. It is! Let me give you a condensed version, and you will see what I mean.

"Each year, on the weekend before Christmas, my side of the family has a large family gathering, sort of like a reunion. I have four brothers and two sisters, and we do not see each other that often, so this has always been a very special time for all of us and our children."

"Angie, why is this special occasion a problem?" I asked.

"Well," she said, "my sister, Bev, and my mother don't get along well at all. In fact, they rarely speak to each other, and when they do, it is best if you are not nearby. The words are very hostile and full of anger. They are both very stubborn, and neither will make any effort to forgive or make up. None of us really even knows what happened to bring them to this point. This has gone on for eight years! We have had no luck trying to intervene. It is so sad because they live 300 miles apart, and it would seem like they would want to enjoy what little time they have together."

Angie continued, "What hurts the most is that the entire atmosphere of our get-together has become so negative that some of the family have said they will no longer attend unless this changes. In fact, I am worried that relatives I look forward to seeing may not even be there this weekend. It is really not a good experience for the grandchildren either. They don't understand what's wrong with Grandma and Aunt Bev. This puts us all in a state of mind that keeps us from enjoying the true meaning of Christmas and this time together as a family."

As Angie finished her story, she became quite emotional. By this time, almost everyone had left the room. Only two ladies were cleaning tables where the food had been. I felt bad for Angie since this situation was obviously making her, her family, and other relatives pretty miserable.

I wish I could tell you this story had a happy ending. Angie had hoped that a reconciliation would take place between Bev and her mother. She prayed that they might find it in their hearts to forgive each other and make up. I don't know if Angie's prayer was ever answered. However, I have heard of similar situations over the years where the differences between friends or relatives were worked out, forgiveness was offered, and the hard feelings came to an end with a joyous celebration.

——◇——

Our ability to love and care for others is greatly reduced when we continue to carry feelings of anger and resentment. What do we gain by recycling these feelings? Bitterness only keeps us bound to the past. Instead, we should move on to restore relationships and regain peace of mind.

> *"Bitterness only keeps us bound to the past."*

Forgiveness can take place at any time, but only if we choose it. It is a gift that we are capable of giving or withholding. When we forgive, it does not mean that we accept or agree with what was done, or that we excuse the other person's responsibility or behavior. With forgiveness, we simply cease to remain angry or resentful toward someone.

Wouldn't it be great to have a National Reconciliation Day, when everyone would make an effort to resolve the issues that tear families, friends, and loved ones apart? But perhaps, more realistically, we could simply establish our own day and take it upon ourselves to mend any uncomfortable, destructive situations that might haunt our own lives. Life is short. Why not let go and forgive?

Much of behavior is learned. We have a wonderful opportunity to teach our children about understanding and forgiveness. Our example speaks louder than words. What do our children see? Do we make quick judgments, or do we listen and try to understand the other person's point of view? Are we willing to change our thinking when it is in error, or does our pride hold us back?

"We have a wonderful opportunity to teach our children about understanding and forgiveness. Our example speaks louder than words."

Forgiveness may be one of the most difficult things we ever do. However, its healing effect can take place immediately and can bring peace even after a friend or loved one has passed away. The sooner forgiveness takes place the better, but it is never too late.

"Those who deny freedom to others deserve it not for themselves."

— Abraham Lincoln

...about freedom

Over the years, I had heard bits and pieces of my good friend Matyas's (Matt) story, but he recently honored me with all the details. As I listened for over two hours, I knew that he shared it as much from his heart as from his memory.

Born in 1933 in a small town in Hungary, Matt had three brothers and three sisters. His father was a farmer. The family endured hard times when the children were young. Because of World War II, the children often missed school; at one point, Matt said he missed half of the school year.

Matt explained how the Communists came to power after the war and combined small farms to create collective farms owned by the government. He did not want to be a farmer all of his life, and he especially did not want to work for a collective farm operated by the Communists. His father was also very opposed to the idea of collective farming because it meant that the Communists would take control of the land.

At the age of 17, Matt went to Veszprem to visit friends and also to look for a job. He learned that one of his friends was attending a trade school. After exploring this option, Matt found a job with a power company that would also provide two years of training and schooling to become an electrician. Matt was to begin his new job soon, but he decided to return home first. When he told his parents about his new job, they were not happy. His mother was okay with it, but his father was quite opposed to him leaving, for he wanted Matt to work their farm.

"When he told his parents about his new job, they were not happy."

"You will become a Communist," his father protested.

But Matt assured his father, "I promise you, I will not become a Communist."

At work, Matt became good friends with a young man who had been raised in an orphanage. As one of their work assignments, they put electricity into a nearby village that had never had power.

Private farmers still were undergoing more and more hardships. When problems arose on the farm at home, including a major fire, Matt went home to help his parents. He was also able to give them some money he had saved. His dad admitted, "This is a good thing that you did." He was happy Matt was learning a trade and would have a different and better life since there really was no future in farming.

Matt told me, "I was happy that I could help them. It made me feel good."

After two years of schooling, Matt graduated and received his diploma. He continued as an electrician with the same company for another year but worked in a different city.

In Hungary, every young man was required to serve in the army, so Matt joined the service for the next two years. After his discharge, he went back to work in an industrial city called Stalinvaros. His new job was interesting, educational, and good paying.

"The Hungarian people wanted things to change; they wanted freedom and independence."

But as fall came, so did turmoil in Hungary. The Hungarian people wanted things to change; they wanted freedom and independence. And so began the uprising and the Hungarian Revolution. Matt and other factory workers gathered and decided that they could not merely sit by; they needed to do something.

Matt's thoughts and those of his friends were about all the great changes they could make for Hungary if only they were free. They had heard many good things about the United States.

"They have running water. And they don't even do dishes," one worker claimed. Matt jokingly told me with a smile, "And it was true. Later when I got to the United States, I saw people eat off of paper plates and then throw them away. And the money to be made in the U.S., wow!"

The Communists felt their way was best; Matt and his coworkers from the factory did not. He and about 1,000 others protested and even asked the police, "How can we protest? How can we demonstrate? We do not want to live under communism." They wanted their independence from Russia. By late that afternoon, their numbers had reached approximately 5,000.

At this point, Matt and many others became freedom fighters. To find out whether the Hungarian Army would support them, many fighters from the group traveled to a nearby Hungarian army post in Stalinvaros to speak with the officers. As they traveled to the post, they carried a Hungarian flag and sang patriotic Hungarian songs.

Matt said, "The citizens supported us in our fight for freedom. We felt we would get our freedom back."

They talked with a general from the Hungarian Army, which was now being controlled by the Russians. Then they waited until after dark to hear whether the army was going to support them or not.

"Suddenly, at 10:00 PM, the Hungarian officers opened fire on us," Matt said. "We hit the ground, went for cover, then took the wounded to the hospital. Two people were killed. A friend I worked with was shot. He was only nineteen," Matt said. "We went to see him the next day. He was dead, but we did get to see his body. He had been shot in the stomach. The uprising in Stalinvaros was the real beginning of the Revolution," Matt pointed out.

"Suddenly, at 10:00 PM, the Hungarian officers opened fire on us."

The next night, 35,000 people protested in the streets to support freedom. Things quieted down a bit, and the Russians pulled back from Budapest for the time being.

Matt said, "We thought that if the Russians saw how much the Hungarian people were united and how badly they wanted their freedom, they would leave. We wanted the Hungarian people to be able to live like the Austrians, free with no more fighting."

Two weeks later when Matt went to Budapest, he saw the total destruction of the city. Russian tanks were everywhere. He decided to go home to his family.

"It was the last time my mother, father, and our family would all be together. We had a good talk," Matt said. He told his family, "No matter what happens, do not worry. What we do is for a good cause. We want Hungarians to be free and to enjoy a good life. We may need to leave the country, but we will keep in touch."

A week later, another surprise came as 350,000 Russian troops moved in to take over Hungary. Matt was now back in Stalinvaros, where he had worked in the factory. Since the revolution, that city has been renamed Dunaujvaros. The factory where Matt worked was closed down for one month. It was very qui-

"It was the last time my mother, father, and our family would all be together."

et, but the Russian troops were coming closer. Matt had to decide what to do. He and other freedom fighters felt they needed to protect their city. They were able to get guns, ammunition, and hand grenades. One of his friends had a small plane and was able to monitor the approaching Russian troops. When

> *"We formed a ring around our city in order to protect it."*

he had to leave the plane, he booby trapped it in case the Communist troops wanted to use it.

"We formed a ring around our city in order to protect it," he said.

"One Russian officer, holding up a white flag, asked to speak to our mayor to see if he would give up Stalinvaros. He would not," Matt said. "The next day the Russian troops began to move in."

Russian jets circled the city and were firing upon it. Matt told his friend they needed to leave right away. Less than two minutes after they jumped into a ditch for cover, an artillery shell hit the exact spot where they had just been. They went to the third floor of their factory and thought they might use a Molotov cocktail to wipe out a communist tank.

"We still wanted to fight for our freedom no matter what happened," Matt said.

"There was gunfire all around us," he explained.

As the Russian tanks moved in, the city's power was cut off, and the factory turned totally dark. There was a curfew, and tanks were evident throughout the town. As dawn came, Matt and his friends changed from their uniforms and were able to walk back home.

"Matt decided that he needed to escape."

"No one could leave," Matt said. "It was a very sad day in late November of 1956."

Matt decided that he needed to escape. His friends tried to talk him out of it.

"What future will you have?" they asked.

"What future do I have here?" Matt responded.

There was chaos for the next month. In December, their factory started up again. Matt and his close friend Imre decided to escape together. They felt that most of the Hungarian escapees would go to Austria.

They planned their escape in much detail. The border between Austria and Hungary had been closed and was heavily patrolled by Russian troops.

Matt and his friend went to visit an old woman who had been his brother's landlady. They had heard she helped people to escape.

"We told her about our plan. We asked her to pray for us," Matt said. Then he paused for a minute and went on, "I will never forget. She put a cross on my forehead, and said, 'Okay, I will pray for you.'"

They asked her what was the best route to escape, and she directed them by way of the small village of Kiszsidany on the border of Austria.

Matt said, "That was what we had thought too. That was our plan."

He explained that a friend's wife Betty had grown up in Kiszsidany and that many times she had described the village to him—the streets, the buildings, the landmarks, and the border.

"I memorized all the details she described," Matt said. "She still had relatives there including a cousin named Joe. We would meet him there."

Matt and Imre left, taking water, sugar, raincoats, and other necessary gear, so they would be able to survive in case they needed to stay hidden for several days. They traveled by train toward a small town closer to the Austrian border and got off the train about ten kilometers short of the town.

"If we went all the way to town, Russian troops would be waiting to check our identification," Matt explained, "and if we were not from that city, they would put us on a truck and haul us away.

"At the stop where we got off, everyone else got off on one side, and we got off on the opposite side so nobody would see us," he said.

> *"'We were not sure of our directions because it was still dark out.'"*

"We were alone and walked across the countryside, never on any main roads. The troops were on the roads, and we would have been picked up. We had to go through open fields. We had a map, but we were confused," he said. "We were not sure of our directions because it was still dark out."

"About 2:00 AM, we came upon another small village. We took another chance and stopped at a house that had a light on. Here we met a Hungarian soldier and his father. We told them the truth and asked for their help," Matt said. "They told us how to get to Kiszsidany by following the tree line through the fields. We thanked them, gave them some money, and left to follow the tree line through the dark mist and rain."

Matt and Imre came upon a long building, a barn from a collective farm. A lone farmer was inside milking a cow. Although they surprised him, he listened as they told him the truth about what they were doing and asked for his help. Exhausted, they asked if they could hide and sleep under his hay for a few hours. They also asked if he would try to see that no one harmed them. The farmer

> *"Exhausted, they asked if they could hide and sleep under his hay for a few hours."*

agreed. They needed to be very careful because if the farmer was caught helping Hungarians escape, the consequences for him and his family would be as drastic as, or worse than, those for Matt and his friend.

After they woke up, the farmer's wife served them breakfast in their home. They gave the farmer and his wife some money, and the couple wished them good luck on their trip. They set off for Kiszsidany to find Joe. They were able to get a ride on a wagon with a man riding through the village. He knew Joe and where he lived.

"He took us to Joe's house," Matt said.

"We told Joe that we knew his cousin Betty and that we wanted to escape," Matt said. "Then we asked him what was the best way."

Joe told them that a gypsy would help them but that they must pay him.

"We talked with the gypsy and made our plans," Matt said. "The gypsy wanted to leave at midnight. I told him no, that we would go at 5:00 AM. It would be dark then and the fog would have come down. It would be harder for the Russian soldiers to see us, and they would be tired from being up all night. This would be the weakest time for them."

The next morning, in the predawn hours of December 16th, 1956, Matt and Imre went to the location where the gypsy had told them to meet. "Four other Hungarians were already there," Matt said. "Six of us would escape together."

"We paid the gypsy 2,000 forints and gave the rest of our money to an old lady. If we were to get killed, at least the money would stay in Hungary," Matt said.

"We trusted the gypsy to take us across the border the best way he knew," Matt continued. "We had to go through a little village and then cross a road. Russian soldiers were patrolling the road every twenty minutes. As soon as it was clear, we moved very quickly, crossing the road and then darting through a back yard and an orchard. We saw a look-out tower ahead. I knew it would be there. I remembered being told that it would be one of our markers.

"The border was now only 1 1/2 kilometers from where we stood. Because we were so close, we had to move very carefully. We went single-file, several feet apart, so the guards would not see us as easily. That is the best way to go," Matt explained.

"We now approached the border and saw where ten to fifteen meters had been cleared out. Before it had been a minefield. We saw footprints. Seeing no soldiers nearby, we knew it was time to go. I will never forget that feeling. I could hear my own heart beat. It is very hard to describe," Matt went on.

"I will never forget that feeling. I could hear my own heart beat."

"We crossed the border! We were in Austria!" Matt exclaimed. "We walked another ten to fifteen feet and sat down. We were all very happy."

"I had written a letter to my folks and gave it to the gypsy to mail to them when he got back to Hungary. In the letter, I told them that I had escaped and was in Austria," he said.

"Just then I heard church bells ring. It was 6:00 AM and we were free.

"It was very foggy, so we simply waited for the sun to come up. That way we could be certain not to accidentally return to Hungary. Many people made the mistake of not knowing where they were in the dark and ended up going back into Hungary," Matt said.

> *"Just then I heard church bells ring. It was 6:00 AM and we were free."*

"My friend and I took over the leadership of our group," Matt went on. "We heard others talking nearby. We needed to move quietly and carefully, so we wouldn't surprise them. We feared they may shoot at us, not knowing we were escapees as they were," he explained. "But we made it safely."

"Two weeks later, no one was able to escape from Hungary," Matt said quietly.

"Austria was a neutral country, and it was prepared to receive the Hungarian refugees," Matt said. "We were first taken to a school where we were fed and then taken by bus to a larger city. Here, many refugees were being housed in an old army building on an American military base. We were fed three meals a day and were given clothing, if needed. We could go to town once a week and were given ten shillings a week to spend.

> *"'Two weeks later, no one was able to escape from Hungary.'"*

"One day close to Christmas, we went to Mauthausen, across the Danube, to visit a concentration camp where 35,000 Jews had been killed," Matt said. "It was such an awful sight to see, simply unbelievable. The place was all fenced in.

"We went into a large building." He continued, "It had many pictures of families who had been killed and plaques that told how many Jews from different nations had died. This was an unforgettable experience, a very sad thing to see. I felt terrible.

"For example," he said, "in one building, there was an oven on steel rollers. There also was a shower room, about thirty feet by thirty feet. The Jewish children and adults would line up outside. The Nazis told them to take off their clothes and gave them a bar of soap. Then they herded them into the shower room. The showers had a water line but also had a gas line," Matt said. "Once a group was in, the gas was turned on. Then the gas was vented out, and the bodies were removed and burned in the oven. It took less than a minute for each extermination. Yet, to kill 35,000 people took a long time, so the Germans made another oven and a bigger gas chamber so that it would not take so long to kill them all.

> *"It made me sick to hear what some human beings did to other human beings."*

"Across the way was a smaller building," Matt hesitated and choked up, "like a butcher shop. There were big tables used for experimental surgery by any doctor who wished. It is very hard to believe what they did. In another nearby building, the Germans shot many of the Jews. They used many different ways to kill them. It was horrible. Very hard to explain," Matt said. "As I listened to the guide tell us about it, it made me sick to hear what some human beings did to other human beings.

"Outside, we saw where people had been killed trying to escape. A barbed wire and electric fence ran along the top of a brick wall. What the Nazis did to the Jewish people was hard to believe. Horrible!" Matt declared.

Matt was very happy that his friend could speak German well and was able to interpret everything that was said during the tour. They had much to think about as they walked the thirty kilometers back to camp.

New Year's was drawing near. Hungarian refugees could go to any non-Communist country which would take them. If they stayed in Europe, they would be close to home in case Hungary later became a free country. Matt and his friend decided to go to England. They were fed well and treated well along the way. The train they boarded made a stop in Germany.

"The Germans wanted us to stay in Germany," Matt said. "I will never forget that."

They continued on their trip and boarded a ship with 800 men; all were Hungarian refugees.

"As the boat took off, it was kind of an emotional experience." Matt paused a bit and said, "We sang the Hungarian National Anthem."

The waters were rough in the English Channel, and Matt and his friend were glad to finally reach England. Next, they went by train to London. On the day they arrived, they signed up to work in the mines. They had to take a physical. They also took classes, including English, and had books to read and copy.

After two months, Matt wanted to find another job and leave the refugee camp. He found a job as an electrician and even had an apprentice who helped him learn English. He told his boss he liked England very much.

"I liked the job, made good money, and rented a room," Matt said.

Matt wrote to his grandfather in the U.S. and also tried to locate his brother Louis. He wanted to go to the United States. People in the American Consulate told Matt that it was possible for him to immigrate to the U.S., but he must apply. He was very discouraged when he found out that there were 18,000 others waiting to leave England, and the wait could be as long as ten to fifteen years.

"I did not give up," Matt said. "I received information from my grandfather and then had to have an interview with the immigration office. They would let me come, sponsored by my grandfather. I was so happy!" he said.

When Matt told the others that he was going to the U.S., he was quite surprised that so many British people also wanted to come to the U.S.

"But these British people have it so good. They live so good, but they still want to go to the U.S.," Matt said. "I wondered, what was this U.S. like—heaven?" he asked, smiling.

"'One hour after I arrived at my hotel, the immigration officer came to my room and gave me my green card.'"

After his interview and physical, the authorities gave approval for Matt to leave for the U.S. He enjoyed London for two more weeks. Then he left on an old four engine plane, which made a stop in Ireland and then flew over Canada on its way to New York.

"One hour after I arrived at my hotel, the immigration officer came to my room and gave me my green card. I could not believe it.

"A few of us who had just arrived wanted to celebrate, but the store would not take my British money for the wine, and the banks were not open every day to exchange money. So, no party," he said.

After a day in New York, Matt boarded a train to Detroit and then to Saginaw, Michigan. His grandfather and grandmother picked him up at the train station.

"I hugged them both," he said. "I was so glad to see them. We rode to their home in Ithaca, which was on an 80 acre farm. I also was able to see my brother Louis.

"It was quite a feeling, arriving in America," he said with a big smile.

Matt was happy to help out on the farm, but he didn't want to be a farmer, so he soon found a job doing electrical work at a local trailer construction company in Alma. For some time, he rode his bike to work carrying his lunch pail, which also contained his dictionary. He became more active in the community, joined a local church, and found a home in Alma. Later, he took a job in the electrical shop of a large factory. He took correspondence classes to improve his English, and he studied American history in order to become an American citizen.

> *"It was quite a feeling, arriving in America."*

"I wanted to become a citizen as soon as I could," he said.

Matt met his wife, Lucy, in Washington DC at the wedding of his brother Louis. One evening, Lucy shared a story of her own. Lucy was from Spain and had been working in Washington for the family of the Chief of Protocol during the Kennedy administration.

Lucy spoke about the time she accompanied the children of the family to a birthday party at the White House for John and Caroline Kennedy.

"I was so excited. It was something special, meeting and shaking hands with President Kennedy and also with Jackie," Lucy said. "The President went to each table and talked to and shook hands with each child and adult in the room. Before he had to leave, he joined us in singing "Happy Birthday."

"Matt and I were married in October. President Kennedy was shot just a few weeks later. It was a very sad time for everyone."

Matt was pleasantly surprised when he heard that his father's request for a visa to visit the U.S. had been approved. He came to visit and stayed for nearly two years. When Matt became a citizen, his father was with him.

"He was happier than I was," Matt said.

As a citizen, Matt could now visit Hungary and return to the U.S. He and Lucy did that and also visited her homeland, Spain.

Matt was later offered a job at the Dow Chemical Company in Midland, Michigan. He had heard so many good things about Dow that he was thrilled to go to work there.

"I was so happy to be working at Dow. I think Dow was happy also," he said. "I had so many good opportunities to learn and so many good experiences that helped me broaden my knowledge in my work," he went on. "Dow was very good in so many ways," Matt said in a proud voice.

"The world underestimates how good the American people really are."

Matt said, "I have met so many fine people. So many have helped me. The world underestimates how good the American people really are. People just don't realize it," he said.

As we finished our time together, Matt admitted that he sometimes misses a Hungarian tradition or two, but he certainly enjoys every bit of being in the United States.

"I enjoy the freedom and the opportunities available to people here. I am very happy and proud to be an American!" he said with a big smile.

———⊰•◇•⊱———

Matt and his wife, Lucy, continue to live in the central Michigan area. They have two married daughters and enjoy every chance they get to spend time with their six wonderful grandchildren. I know of no one who enjoys Michigan's great hunting and fishing more than Matt does.

After Matt had been in the U.S. for 25 years, he and Lucy invited 300 friends to help celebrate the occasion with a pig roast. They were overwhelmed that so many people came to celebrate the special time with them.

The local newspaper published an article titled, "Hungarian Freedom Fighter: Glad to Be an American." It appeared in The Gratiot County Herald on September 11th of 1982.

I often wonder what it is about freedom that allows us to so easily take it for granted. As we cross paths with those who might not value their citizenship or treasure their freedom, perhaps, we could tell them of stories like Matt's and those of many others. We could also remind them of the many American soldiers who have been killed in the line of duty, the thousands of heroic veterans who have served our country, and the dedicated men and women in our armed services who work to defend and protect our freedom today.

As I write, it is nearing Christmas. It would be very appropriate if we treasured our freedom as one of the most valuable gifts we will ever receive.

"A hundred years from now it will not matter what my bank account was, the sort of house I lived in, or the kind of car I drove…but the world may be different because I was important in the life of a child."

— *Forest E. Witcraft*

...about priorities

I sat on the carpet in the family room playing a game with my five-year-old grandson. Just as I made my move, the phone rang. When I answered, my wife, Helen, said, "Turn on the TV. A plane just crashed into the World Trade Center."

Yes, the date was September 11, 2001. I remember where I was and what I was doing that day as clearly as the day President John F. Kennedy was shot. Our memories have a way of storing events like these forever. Perhaps, it is because we find them to be so tragic and unimaginable.

As I turned on the television, I saw the World Trade Center's north tower in flames. It was not yet 9:00 AM. Within minutes, I saw another airliner strike the south tower. Less than an hour passed when the news came that another hijacked plane had crashed into the Pentagon. Later, we heard of a fourth airliner that had crashed into a field near Shanksville, Pennsylvania because several brave passengers helped divert its course. By doing so, they saved what may have been hundreds of lives. Those passengers thought and acted quickly and unselfishly.

Though I watched the news coverage throughout the day, the true impact of these horrific events did not hit me until later in the day. It seemed too unbelievable. How could thousands of innocent victims be slaughtered in a matter of minutes by such senseless acts of hatred? Nearly 3,000 people were needlessly killed, including citizens from over thirty countries. America suffered an enormous loss.

We, in the United States, have always felt secure. Isn't terrorism something that happens somewhere else? But on that day, our feelings of safety left us, and it may be years before we feel safe again. We discovered a new enemy on American soil, and throughout this country our lives changed forever.

"We discovered a new enemy on American soil, and throughout this country our lives changed forever."

This change was especially true for those who were directly involved. As we all know, thousands of courageous heroes helped in many different ways, saving countless lives.

Those who witnessed the event said it was far worse than anything we saw on television. They felt totally helpless. Imagine seeing innocent people jumping from buildings because they felt it was their best alternative or looking across blocks of debris and finding clothing strewn in the rubble. No doubt thousands have felt, "There but for the grace of God go I."

"Those who witnessed the event said that it was far worse than anything we saw on television."

I ended September 11th by going to church. On my way, I passed several other churches; all were having services to honor the innocent victims and to pray for their grieving families. At our church we prayed, lit candles, and sang hymns for those who had died and for their loved ones. We also gave encouragement to one another. As the day drew to a close, millions of people in this country and around the world were struggling with the unbelievable events of the day.

As I went to bed, I thought of all the children who had lost parents that day; the children numbered about 2,000. I pictured them gathering around the table for their evening meal. There would be an empty chair where their mom or dad had sat earlier that morning at breakfast. When they went to bed that night, they would not hear the usual, "I love you," from that parent, nor would they ever hear it again. I remember seeing their solemn faces in the news photos of their parents' funerals, and I wondered about the fairness of it all. But life is not always fair.

Many of us may still feel anger and hatred toward those who carried out those criminal acts. These and other emotions are normal as long as they are not directed in a hostile or negative manner. As we remember the events and continue to discuss them with others, including our children, we need to show concern and compassion rather than anger and revenge.

"Since that day, we have seen an outpouring of support from across America and from around the world."

Since that day, we have seen an outpouring of support from across America and from around the world. Great sympathy and compassion have been shown toward the families and the surviving victims. We have heard many heartwarming stories of love and heroism. We all remember the loving messages that came from people on the flights or in the towers to their loved ones back home. We have seen more hugging, more prayers, more blood donations, more flags flying, and more young people joining the military.

As a result of 9/11, a shift in thinking began to take place. People's lives took on new perspectives, and they began to reevaluate their priorities. Many decided that their careers and professional aspirations would take second place to their families and loved ones. Some were inspired to make major career changes where their work would help people and contribute to a better world.

People began to look at life on a grander scale. Little inconveniences and everyday problems became quite insignificant. People became more grateful for their loved ones and friends. They realized they loved their families more than anything, and they began to spend more time with them. One individual spoke of hugging his wife and children and feeling so thankful that they were all together because for so many others that was not the case. People took less for granted and felt blessed and thankful for what they had.

"Little inconveniences and everyday problems became quite insignificant."

Freedom was one blessing that was often mentioned. Some people spoke of our American society as one of opportunity, as well as freedom, and mentioned that this was not true in the homelands that their parents had left. Others spoke of the pride they felt for America and the new awareness they had for the price of freedom. 9/11 has helped people realize what is important. In this way, some good may have come from that tragic day.

"In this way, some good may have come from that tragic day."

September 11, 2001 has taught us many lessons regarding mortality, love, priorities, and freedom. These should never be forgotten; however, we often fall back into our old ways of thinking. Our culture and society tend to place great value on success and wealth, and it is easy to get caught up in them. These things are not bad in and of themselves, but we need to find a proper balance of them in our lives, for they are not the things that bring true happiness.

We need to distinguish the difference between our wants and needs. Peace of mind does not come from having everything we want but comes from being satisfied with what we have. We need to remember that the most important things in life are not "things."

As we refocus our priorities, we might try worrying less about the grades of our children, the cleanliness of our houses, the ages of our cars, the weeds in our lawns, the brand names of our clothes, and even the leaks in our roofs. Instead, we may want to pay more attention to the people in our lives, the values of our children, the patience we have with the elderly, the compassion we show to the sick, and the help we give to the poor.

> *"Peace of mind does not come from having everything we want but comes from being satisfied with what we have."*

Tragic events like 9/11 force us to develop a new sense of urgency about our relationships and a greater awareness of how fragile life really is. We realize that every day we have above ground is a gift. Tomorrow is not promised. We only have today.

It would be appropriate if we would recognize September 11th each year and pay a quiet tribute to those who lost their lives and to the families they left behind. We would be honoring their lives, not their deaths. It could be a special day for us to pause and reflect on our priorities. We are different now.

These events have changed our lives. I believe they have made us a more loving and caring people, and as such, our country and world will be a better place. As a nation of resilient people, we will continue to grow stronger and closer. We are united now more than ever in our desire to preserve our freedom. We understand that freedom is never free. In fact, it is priceless.

" Now faith is the substance of things hoped for, the evidence of things not seen. "

— Hebrews 11:1

...about faith

There were no windows in the room, and the lights had been turned down; there was no need for bright lights, for we were simply there to talk, share, listen and learn. It was a large, attractive, comfortable room. Scenic photographs hung on the walls. A picture of Christ also hung on one wall, and a large simple cross graced the front of the room.

I had been attending a three-day conference along with about forty other men and women. It was a wonderful opportunity to relax, quiet ourselves, and reflect on certain aspects of our lives, which we seldom take the time to do. The quiet atmosphere gave us a real chance to spend time with ourselves without the constant interruptions that occur in our daily lives. During the three days, we could attend services or topical sessions, listen to special speakers, enjoy fine meals, and spend as much quiet time alone as we wished.

On the third day, nearing the end of our time together, our gathering was to be a time of reflection on what we had learned or experienced during the retreat. It was an opportunity to share if we wished. We were seated on comfortable chairs so we could see each other. A few men and women offered positive insights about the sessions and speakers. Several others shared experiences that strengthened their faith or brought them new energy to tackle their problems with greater conviction. It was also heartwarming to hear a couple of teenagers make powerful comments about what they gained through their positive experiences.

As our session drew to a close, a lady on the other side of the room stood up. We had been in a couple of the same sessions together. She began by saying, "My name is Kathy, and I attend these conferences as often as I can. I know it is my own responsibility to keep myself motivated and to keep my faith active and growing. I am a grandmother, and I have a short story to tell."

"Several others shared experiences that strengthened their faith or brought them new energy to tackle their problems with greater conviction."

The room was quiet. A few people looked surprised, perhaps that this lady could in fact be a grandmother. We listened carefully as she spoke.

"First, I must tell you that I have a wonderful son, Joe, and he has a fantastic wife whose name is Ann. They live in southern Indiana. They have a little girl named Jenni. Of course, this little girl, my only grandchild, is the most special child in the world to me, as your grandchildren are to you, I know.

"I want to tell you about Jenni. She is five and attends kindergarten in a religious school. She loves it, and the staff is wonderful. This is her third year because she attended preschool there for two years.

"She has been in my thoughts and prayers for the past three years. Since she was two, she has had serious problems with an asthmatic condition. It had not gotten better, even with all the new medications and treatments and with all the wonderful care from her doctors. She had missed a great deal of her kindergarten experience. In fact her asthmatic condition had been so bad that she had stopped going to school. She had been so sick that she had a very difficult time even climbing up a few steps," Kathy said.

"The doctors were baffled," Kathy told us. "They finally recommended that Joe and Ann take her to a special children's hospital to see a specialist. Needless to say, we were all very concerned, and her parents were ready to panic. They thought and prayed about it and agreed that before they would make an appointment at the hospital, they would try something else."

As Kathy continued, her voice cracked a bit, but her expression remained confident.

"Joe and Ann talked to Jenni's teacher and principal, and they asked if they could bring Jenni to school, even though she was ill and had not been in school for over three weeks. They were told they could bring her in for part of a morning. When Jenni arrived at school with her parents, everyone was very happy to see her. The children were especially thrilled to see Jenni, and they let her know how happy they were that she was there.

"'The children were especially thrilled to see Jenni, and they let her know how happy they were that she was there.'"

"Jenni talked to some of the children for a few minutes. Then she was seated in the center of a large carpeted area, and all of the children sat around her in a circle. The teacher shared with the class that Jenni and her mom and dad would like it very much if they would pray together for

Jenni to get better and be able to come back to school. The children all agreed and thought it would be a good thing to do. Prayer was not hard for them. They did it as a part of every day," Kathy said.

"It took just a minute as the teacher lead a prayer. As a part of the prayer, each child could say a few words if they wished. Several of them did," Kathy said.

"Please help Jenni get better," one little girl said softly.

"God, we want Jenni here in school. Please make her get well," a small boy said.

And another little girl said, "Please help Jenni get rid of this thing that makes her sick."

After they were done with the prayers, the teacher asked the children, "Would you like to just go over to Jenni and quietly and gently put your hand on her head and tell her that you want her to get better and come back to school?"

"As part of the prayer, each child could say a few words if they wished. Several of them did."

"Without a word or hesitation, each of them stood, formed a line, and began to go over to Jenni. They placed their hands on her head, spoke a few words, some softly and others loudly as children do, and then sat back down," Kathy explained.

"I wasn't there," Kathy said. "But Joe and Ann said it was the most moving experience they had ever witnessed.

"Jenni's face lit up. She was so happy to be there with her friends, and she told them so. She thanked her teacher for letting her come. Both of her parents and her teacher watched Jenni. They seemed to see a new energy come to her. She walked more effortlessly as she left the room holding her parents' hands. When they went out the front door of the school, Jenni asked if she could go down the steps alone. Shocked but willing to let her try, both Joe and Ann watched with amazement and joy as she stepped slowly and carefully down the steps using only the hand rail. She managed the same steps that an hour earlier would have been impossible for her.

> *"She managed the same steps that an hour earlier would have been impossible for her."*

"Jenni's health seemed markedly improved. Her asthmatic attacks became far less frequent, and her symptoms decreased at a noticeable rate. After about a week, she returned to school and has had very few absences since."

Kathy was obviously moved by this experience of her granddaughter. Though it was emotional for her to tell it, she wanted to share the story with us.

"What better example could we have than the faith of small children?"

"I thank God that Jenni is doing so much better and that she attends school regularly. She loves school. I am also very thankful that I have a son and daughter-in-law with a very strong faith."

Kathy closed by saying, "You have been very patient. Thanks for listening to my story."

After a moment, several people thanked Kathy for sharing her story. As we concluded our meeting, the leader of the group said, "Perhaps this is a most fitting ending to our three-day experience. We came here for a tune-up to our lives and our faith. What better example could we have than the faith of small children?"

A friend of mine recently said he found it hard to understand how we could not see God in everything around us.

"It is so obvious," he said, "in the millions of examples of His creation all around us, in the birds, the flowers, in all of nature, and especially in the birth of a child."

We need to recognize the tremendously important spiritual aspect that exists in the very being of each of us and also acknowledge the results that can come from faith in God.

"Every gun that is made, every warship launched, every rocket fired, signifies in the final sense a theft from those who hunger and are not fed, those who are cold and are not clothed."

— *Dwight D. Eisenhower*

...about hunger & homelessness

Over the last few years, I have read quite a bit about the hunger problem in America and around the world. The more I have learned, the more interested I've become. I wanted to understand the problem better, so I decided to spend some time visiting several soup kitchens, food pantries, rescue missions, and homeless shelters.

My good friend Father Bob is a chaplain at a soup kitchen in a large Midwestern city. His work reminds me so much of what Jesus did when hundreds gathered to hear Him, but no food was available except for a few loaves of bread and a few fish. Jesus recognized the hunger and the shortage of food. His heart went out to the people, and He met their need for food. He multiplied the loaves and fishes until there was enough food for everyone. Father Bob spends most of his waking hours modeling that behavior on behalf of the poor, hungry, and homeless. Hundreds of men, women, and children receive well balanced, nutritious meals at the kitchen every day.

I had the wonderful opportunity of meeting numerous "guests" at the soup kitchen and at the rescue mission. I ate breakfast, lunch, and dinner with many of them. I was able to listen to their stories and study their faces. I also spent time with a few of them during several short church services which Father Bob conducted in a church about a block from the soup kitchen.

The soup kitchen and rescue mission were very impressive; they were clean and operated in an efficient and orderly fashion. Of course, they met all the necessary health department requirements. No questions were asked of the guests, and no judgments were made about them. Each person who came for a meal was fed. Many made use of other services such as showers, clean clothing, support services, bus passes, and other help that they may have needed.

"I was able to listen to their stories and study their faces."

I asked Father Bob if they always had enough food and he said, "Yes, at least so far." There was no doubt that the food sources were reliable and provided high quality food. Staff members at the kitchen and rescue mission appeared to be sensitive, caring people. They were obviously there to help others, as were the many volunteers who helped to serve and clean up after the meals. On one of the days I visited the rescue mission, girls from a local Girl Scout Troop had volunteered to help.

I would like to share with you several fascinating stories about the interesting, wonderful people I met.

"Winter is one of the greatest enemies of the poor."

Joe grew up in a large city and later moved to northern Michigan where he attended college and was married. He and his wife had a family together, and he ran a successful business. However, after an accident, he was unable to work as before. Joe now lived on the streets and spent his time looking for returnable bottles and cans when he was not at the soup kitchen eating his meals and visiting with friends. He often slept under a bridge, except for the coldest part of the winter when he would look for a homeless shelter that had room for him. Joe's health was now failing, and Father Bob was quite concerned that he might not make it through the winter if he did not get into a shelter. Winter is one of the greatest enemies of the poor. This past winter, Joe was able to stay at the NSO, Neighborhood Services Organization. Joe had a very bad case of lice and also a very strong body odor. He was offered a shower and clean clothing, but he declined.

Karl had a warrant out for his arrest; he had recently violated the conditions of his parole. Karl grew up in a large city and had lived there all his life except for the time he spent in prison. He appeared to be a healthy man. He walked about an hour to get to the soup kitchen. Three days a week, Karl was picked up at 5:00 AM and taken to dialysis, where he spent three hours at a time. After dialysis, his ride dropped him off at the soup kitchen. He was happy about that. Karl currently lived at a shelter. He said, "The shelter fills up real quick, especially when the weather gets cold."

Kathy obviously had a deep faith. I met her at one of Father Bob's church services. She carried a very worn and tattered Bible. She told me she would write her story and send it to me. I hope she does.

The church services were conducted in such a manner that those attending could participate and share if they wished. When I was there, about ten to fifteen people attended. They shared their thoughts, beliefs, and experiences. It was obvious that faith played a major role in the lives of these people. The services also provided a warm, comfortable place to spend a little time with friends. It was far better than being on the street and provided much needed contact with others.

Larry and I met one day as he was getting off of his bike. He wanted to talk, so we sat for a while, and he told me a bit about himself. He lived on the outskirts of a small community. Actually, he lived in a storage unit. "I like it better here than where I was before. There, people were drunk or would steal from me," he said. "I don't worry about that now."

"It was obvious that faith played a major role in the lives of these people."

Larry had spent fifteen years in the service but had no income from there and was too young for Social Security. He did receive some money because of a disability, so he could pay the $40.00 rental fee on the unit and have a little money for food and other necessities. We parted because Larry needed to get a few things from a store, and he wanted to ride the six miles back to his unit before it was too dark.

Jason's view about hunger and homelessness was entirely different from most of the others. He felt the whole thing was based upon the need and/or desire for freedom. He explained, "These people want to live this way. For them, it's a choice. Many of them are really not hungry. Several give their food away. Look at them. As you can see, several are overweight. They come here to socialize." Jason was a fairly bright young man in his early 20's. Perhaps, he was describing his own situation and was generalizing and projecting his perception on a broader population.

"I was only twelve years old when I found my mom dead in bed. She was a diabetic. She was also a heroin addict. The needle was still in her arm," Marcy said softly with tears in her eyes. We were having lunch together on a cold December day at the soup kitchen. She went on to tell me more of her chaotic life as a child and why she now depended upon the soup kitchen for her meals.

"I was only twelve years old when I found my mom dead in bed."

When Carmen and I ate breakfast, she told me, "Some of these people do have some type of a job but come here to eat, so they can make ends meet. Then they don't have to spend as much money on food since they get good meals here. They can use it for rent, utilities, and other things. Sometimes that might include drugs." Carmen had a six-year-old son, whom she had not seen in two years. "They came to get him. I don't know where he is now," she said. She also expressed much concern about being hurt and robbed on the street.

Clyde said he had always lived in the big city. His dad worked in the steel mills. Clyde still lived with his parents, but he did some work as a painter and repairman to make a few dollars. He, too, ate at the soup kitchen in order to save his money for other things.

As we finished our dinner one evening, Ann told me, "I have thought about suicide several times." Ann had grown up in the big city but was now living in a smaller town. She was eating at the rescue mission and sleeping in a nearby shelter for the time being. Staff at the mission were also providing Ann with some basic job skills and were working with her to find a job. She had no family and her only friends were ones she had made at the mission and shelter.

"I had it all," Andy told me. "A nice wife, two great kids, a good job, nice home, everything. Together, we made about

$60,000 a year. I could pull anything from the fridge and sit down and eat with my family in a nice warm home."

Andy thought he could handle alcohol and not become addicted like others did, but he was wrong. He was arrested for abuse and spent thirty days in jail. As a result, he lost his job and family.

"This has made me humble," he said. Sometimes, Andy slept in shelters. He said, "Often when you sleep, you need to get up early and leave. It can be very dangerous."

Andy had a new room but said it was filthy like a sewer. He carried everything he owned in a backpack.

"Andy thought he could handle alcohol and not become addicted like others did, but he was wrong."

He said, "I am on my way back. I am trying hard to stay away from alcohol. I am looking for a job and have some interviews." I hope he is successful.

Father Bob told me of a mentally-ill lady who lived in a rooming house in a room that was more like a coal bin. Light was provided by one dim bulb. She did have food available, and others in the house were supposed to care for her and fix her meals. They did fix the meals, but then they ate them. One time, Father Bob and a friend delivered a bed to her. She was incontinent; her old bed reeked with the strong smell of urine, and the springs were rusted through in places. Once, she had gone to the hospital for several days, and when she returned, the landlord had rented her room. From then on, he let her sleep in a chair in the lobby and charged her rent.

"I gave up all three of my children. I knew I could not be a good mom."

One of the people I will never forget is Glynda who, like Joe, had lived on the streets for the better part of two years. She had her first child when she was just fifteen. She said she also began her drug addiction about that time. "I gave up all three of my children. I knew I could not be a good mom." Glynda was about 45 years old and she was still an addict. During those thirty years, she had been in several treatment programs, but she was still unable to break her habit. She had also been in several training programs but was not able to maintain successful employment.

Glynda told me about the time she went to the home of her sister and brother-in-law and asked if she could sleep in their garage or in their car. They told her no. She then asked if they would take her to the hospital emergency room and they refused again. The hospital would have found a shelter for her. She asked if she could use their phone to call the hospital and was again rejected.

On this cold February night, Glynda had hauled a refrigerator box for over a mile to use as a shelter under a bridge. She'd had to fight to keep the box because others had tried to take it from her. She and a few others usually kept a fire burning in a barrel, so they could have some heat.

"It's very dangerous out there," she said. "You must watch everything you do. Be careful when you sleep. Hide your food. Watch when you eat it. People want your food. They will bully you and steal it from you. I saw a man get beaten badly for half a can of pop."

Glynda also told me about the many times she had eaten sandwiches from a dumpster. She and others like her know the exact days and times when the restaurants and grocery stores put unused food and waste into the dumpsters.

As we finished our lunch, Glynda also told me how her hunger felt sometimes.

"I lie there all night and can feel my stomach touch my backbone. But I know I can get up in the morning and walk over here for coffee and a good breakfast. If it were not for this soup kitchen, several of these people would not be alive today," she said, as she looked around the room at the people.

> *"I lie there all night and can feel my stomach touch my backbone."*

With all that Glynda had been through in the past thirty years, I found her an intelligent, verbal, and still quite attractive lady with a very strong faith. She still wanted to finish her GED. "I try hard to be kind to others, to stay healthy, and to do what is right," she said.

I spoke with a number of other people who were living on the streets. They felt that it was not so bad in good weather. A few of them carried sleeping bags in plastic bags. Several others said that if it rains, they head for shelter in a nearby bus station. One man slept in an abandoned bus in an alley. He was embarrassed and did not want people to know this. Another young man slept in a deserted camper in a field, and another slept in a tent. Like Glynda with the refrigerator box, some said they had gotten a box from a washer or dryer and placed it over a grate for heat. It is common to see many of these homeless people carrying plastic bags full of their belongings. They may also carry paper bags, backpacks, or duffel bags. Sometimes a man or a woman pushes an old grocery cart containing everything they own. The cart not only contains the items but makes them much easier to transport. Some people may have a locker, perhaps at a shelter, but even then they run the risk of things being stolen.

Stealing is common. Stolen items often include food, shoes, blankets, diapers, or a bag of someone's belongings, the contents of which are unknown to the thief. One upset woman said someone had recently stolen her Bible. Often the items are sold in order to maintain survival. A woman may wear a small purse under a sweatshirt which will help her in shoplifting or getting food for her small children. For many, food stamps do not provide enough money for the food they need.

"For many, food stamps do not provide enough money for the food they need."

Though a number of hungry and homeless people receive checks from Social

Security, their other income is very limited. A small amount of income may come from recyclable bottles and cans which are found on the streets, in empty lots, or in garbage cans. Sometimes items are sold, including food items from the soup kitchen. Selling blood at a local plasma center is also not uncommon.

"Many of them not only lose their identity, they lose their self-esteem and frequently become depressed."

Many drug and alcohol addicts are among the hungry and homeless. Some are former mental patients, unemployed people, and young runaways. Others have lost their homes for various reasons such as fires, floods, tornadoes, and sometimes eviction.

Finding suitable, affordable housing is a major problem; there is simply not enough available. The homeless are in a difficult position, for without an address, there is no way to get help, support, or public assistance. Homeless people are hard to identify and to count. Many of them not only lose their identity, they lose their self-esteem and frequently become depressed. They often face a sad reality when filling out papers and applications. They simply leave the space blank after "Who to contact in an emergency." They have no one.

So many people are constantly looking for a shelter or place to live. Some people have been living this way for years. Many just keep returning to the same shelters. These offer very little privacy. Sometimes, a large number of people sleep in the same room, and they may have to share a shower or bathroom down the hall. A couple of men claimed that drug abuse and stealing go on in some of the shelters. Most believe that the shelters provided by the churches are safer. Several churches provide a 24-hour drop-in center and allow clients to use the name and address of the church, so they can claim government assistance, food stamps, and other help.

I found that homeless people are very street smart. When one lives on the street, one finds ways to communicate very well. It does not take long to find out where and when free meals are available. One learns where to get support services and assistance, where to go for bus passes, and also where to find clean clothing and showers, if possible.

It is difficult for homeless people to maintain personal hygiene and a proper appearance. They will probably be on the streets most of the day, every day. The streets have no toilets or showers. What can they do? On the one hand, a person should be clean and look presentable when going to an appointment or possible job interview, but on the other hand, that may be very hard to accomplish under the circumstances. Also, transportation to interviews and other appointments may be difficult to find or schedule.

It is not uncommon for people living on the streets to consider suicide. They worry about crime, violence, prostitution, drug abuse, sexual

"It is not uncommon for people living on the streets to consider suicide."

assault, and possible personal injury. During winter months, people have to walk home from the soup kitchen in the dark, which can be very dangerous. There are also confrontations with the police. People on the streets are often lonely, depressed, and fearful of the conditions around them.

I found it unfortunate that many homeless people keep to themselves and seem to have few friends. They are embarrassed and humiliated by the situation they find themselves in. Still, they are a proud people and do not like to ask for help because they feel people will judge them as being lazy, addicted, or incompetent. But they learn to trust a few select people and will ask them for help. So many are in great need. Many are ill and even dying.

We must also consider the many children who are on the streets. They are usually with a parent or another adult. They probably stay in a room in a shelter with no privacy, may lack proper nutrition, and may have no place to study or do homework. They may, in fact, not have a regular school because of their unstable lives. In some cases, the mother may suffer from depression. AIDS may have taken the life of a parent, relative, or friend. For others, their fathers may be in prison. In spite of the conditions, nearly all of the children I saw in the soup kitchen, rescue mission, and shelters were well-behaved and seemed to be happy and optimistic.

> *"The last thing a child should have to worry about 24 hours a day is food and shelter."*

With all the negative conditions that exist in the lives of so many children, should we wonder why some do poorly in school? They need constant love, assurance, and much more stability in their lives. The last thing a child should have to worry about 24 hours a day is food and shelter. Perhaps it is a miracle that many do well and are so resilient.

Father Bob reminded me that the problems of the poor, including the hungry and homeless, are very complex issues. Many of the children are not homeless but live in clearly substandard housing. That often means no heat, no electricity, and even no water in many cases. The bigger picture involves sociological issues, unemployment, drug and alcohol dependency, and, for certain, issues of low self-esteem. In many cases, there may be a personal history of abusive behavior or abuse. Not to be overlooked is the fear of responsibility and even the fear of success. Even though depression, fear, and uncertainty fill the thoughts of many of these people, a bit of cheerfulness, maturity, and hope often did shine through.

> *"A bit of cheerfulness, maturity, and hope often did shine through."*

Most of the people I met were quite appreciative of all that was being done for them. The soup kitchen, rescue mission, and shelters offer a tremendous service to hundreds of people in need. Their services go far beyond simply serving food but include many other personal and social services. The nearby food bank distributes 250,000 pounds of food each month. In addition to these, I learned that there are many other caring people and wonderful resources in many communities that provide food, shelter, medical assistance, treatment programs, life skills, and basic job training to those in need. Numerous churches offer a variety of services.

Much of what I have shared about hunger and homelessness is not new information. Many of us have known it all along. It is simply not something that crosses our minds regularly. As we all well know, this problem exists not only in large cities but in many urban areas, midsize towns, and even small communities in our country. Is there more we can do than simply feel compassion? Perhaps, we need to develop and strengthen our moral courage.

"Is there more we can do than simply feel compassion?"

Although I have never experienced poverty, I do remember my family trying to scrape together enough change to buy a loaf of bread when I was a child. Bread cost 18 cents at the time. Things might have been tight, but I don't ever remember going hungry, and I don't believe we ever considered ourselves to be poor. I am truly thankful I was born to the parents I had in this wonderful country.

Many people around us are trying to lose weight, so it's hard to understand how hunger could be a problem. But hunger and poverty are real in our country and throughout the world. We may believe that hunger exists because there is a shortage of food, but many sources claim that we are capable of producing enough food to feed everyone in the world, now and in the future. The intellectual know-how and the technical ability certainly exist.

It may seem as though the solution to hunger should not be that difficult, but many factors complicate the problem. Religion, race, ethnic conflicts, and violence can all be contributing factors. Often it is due to poor governmental policies, political controls, and inappropriate priorities within a country. For example, farmland may lie idle because of government intervention. Food may be ex-

"Hunger and poverty are real in our country and throughout the world."

ported for higher profits. In one country, fish was exported for dog and cat food instead of being used to feed the hungry at home. Also, foreign aid may not be used where it is intended. Money and power may take priority over the welfare of the people. Most studies show that democratic, free market countries tend to consider the needs of their people more. When a concerned government receives aid, we can count on it being used as it was intended. Where hunger is a priority, progress can be made.

Positive steps are being taken to alleviate world hunger through education, especially in Third World countries. People are being taught how to properly plant, grow, and harvest their food in order to help them become more self-sufficient. Credit certainly must be given to the hundreds of dedicated organizations around the world that work very hard to bring an end to this problem.

Yet, much still needs to be done. Hunger may not be in the headlines, but it is still present on our streets and the streets of countless other countries. Accurate figures of deaths due to hunger are not available. Even though hunger may not be life threatening in many cases, there are many hunger-related illnesses that attack and weaken the immune system. Therefore, hunger may be the indirect cause of many deaths. If more data were available, perhaps it would increase the public and political desire to do more.

Human beings are our greatest resource, and children are our future. Children cannot learn on empty stomachs or with burdened minds. They are the most vulnerable. The poor have little power. They are often treated as though they don't matter or even exist. They need our help to move beyond these circumstances. An evil like hunger can only exist when people and governments choose to turn their heads and look the other way. Unless the lives of poor people are considered to be as important and sacred as yours and mine, things will not change. Where human life is truly valued, all people will be treated as equals, with respect and concern.

"Children cannot learn on empty stomachs or with burdened minds."

The needs of poverty-stricken Americans and others around the world must become a moral priority. Let us all consider how our abilities and resources can help. We must cooperatively work to bring hunger to an end.

"Appreciation is a wonderful thing: It makes what is excellent in others belong to us as well."

— Voltaire

…about appreciation

The snow was as deep as I had ever seen it; nearly thirty inches had fallen. It was almost 6:00 PM and though it was very cloudy, it was still light. It had finally stopped snowing, and the heavy winds had died down. Each step that I took was very difficult because I had to lift my entire leg and foot up out of the snow to move it ahead a step. I had about a quarter-mile to go before I reached the house where Frank and Minnie lived.

Most of the main roads had been plowed but not the road where our friends Frank and Minnie lived. They were a brother and a sister living on their old family homestead a few miles out of town. Minnie was an "old maid" and Frank had been a bachelor all of his life.

Their older bachelor brother, Ed, had passed away a year or two before we met them. The three siblings had worked very hard managing the old farm that their parents had worked for many years. Horses had pulled the farm equipment to do most of the work in the past. Only in recent years had Frank and Minnie acquired some new farming equipment. They still owned their hay mower and baler and had an old but well maintained tractor. But now that Ed was gone and with Frank and Minnie getting up in years, they leased their land to a neighboring family to farm.

Frank, however, still loved to do a little farming when he could. That is where my family comes into the picture. We owned a very small farm with a few acres just down the road from Frank and Minnie's home. Both of our girls had beautiful Morgan horses named Penny and Lu. We raised hay for the horses and hired Frank to mow and to bale it for us. He was very knowledgeable and reliable. He knew the importance of timing and weather when it came to cutting, raking, and baling hay. Getting the hay up in the barn was an important goal; when our hay was up, we were all happy.

> *"Frank still loved to do a little farming when he could."*

We became quite good friends with Frank and Minnie. We checked on them regularly and helped them with their yard work and other tasks. Since much of their heating and all of their cooking were done with wood, I chopped wood for them, and the girls stacked it in the entryway of the old farmhouse. Other friends and neighbors were also there to help on numerous occasions.

As the years went by, both Frank's and Minnie's health began to deteriorate. Frank couldn't do as much, and Minnie was not able to cook and handle household chores very well. The doctor recommended that, for health and nutritional reasons, Frank and Minnie should get Meals-on-Wheels. This included a hot dinner for each of them and a sack lunch for the next day, which were prepared and distributed by our local hospital about five miles away.

These meals were usually delivered by volunteers within the city limits, but in our area the volunteer services did not include taking meals to people that lived out in the country. So my wife and I took on the responsibility of picking these meals up at the hospital each afternoon and taking them to Frank and Minnie. This task only took a few minutes each day, and we enjoyed the opportunity to visit with them when we delivered the meals. My wife and I were both from the city, so it was a wonderful opportunity for us to learn about life in the early years on their Centennial Farm.

But snowy days like this provided a real test for us. On this particular day, I was barely able to get to their house through the deep snow. Frank had cleared some of the snow away from the doorway so that I could get into the entryway of their home. They were expecting me, but later they admitted that they had their doubts that I could get through.

I was very happy to finally reach their door and get into the house. As I stomped my feet and brushed the snow from my coat and pants, I could see the glint of appreciation in Minnie's eyes. It was a scene I will never forget. As they sat at their kitchen table, I saw the warmest smiles and happiest faces I have ever seen on anyone. Removing her old wire-rimmed glasses to wipe a tear or two, Minnie said, "We are so glad to see you. Thank you so much for bringing our meals. We did not think you would make it today."

That day I learned what true appreciation really means. I certainly received many other smiles and thank-yous from Frank and Minnie over the years, but none remains clearer in my mind than the one I received on that blustery February day. These two people had become very independent, having lived through war, depression, and many other personal and family hardships. But at the same time, they remained very caring and generous people who were always ready to help a neighbor in need, and they were humble and appreciative when someone did something for them.

We were fortunate to know Frank and Minnie until they passed away a few years later. These fine people found a way to give even after they were gone. Through their generosity, a special scholarship fund was established in their names at the local high school. Many young people have benefited from their generosity, and many more will continue to do so in the future.

"Many young people have benefited from their generosity and many more will continue to do so in the future."

Frank and Minnie understood the importance of neighbors helping one another. They gave whenever they could and were most gracious and thankful in accepting help from others when it was needed. This give-and-take relationship benefited us all, and we never minded giving because we knew our help would always be appreciated. That was enough.

As we look around us each day, we need to pay attention to the many helpful deeds that come our way. These acts of kindness should be repaid with our appreciation. We should never take anything for granted—not the big things, not the small things, and most of all, not the special people in our lives.

"The best part of beauty is that which no picture can express."

— *Francis Bacon*

...about beauty

"Wow, is she stunning!" came a voice from the doorway of my office.

I looked up from my desk and saw Jake, a good friend and colleague with whom I had worked for several years.

"Good morning, Jake," I replied. "It sounds like you've just met our new receptionist."

"Yes, I did," he said. "Who is she?"

"Her name is Julie. She came to us from the employment agency as a temporary. You remember Beth? She resigned pretty unexpectedly, so we needed someone to fill in right away. Julie came to us about a week ago. She is doing a fine job."

"She certainly was pleasant when I came in, and her big smile made me feel welcome. You know, I have seen some very attractive women in my day, but she certainly ranks at the top. Like I said, she is simply stunning," Jake repeated.

"You're right, she is. She also has a great personality, and a very good work ethic. I really do hope we are able to keep her as the receptionist," I continued. "She has already learned a great deal about our organization and has been a big help to many clients."

Several months went by, and I was able to get to know Julie better. Julie liked to stay busy. Often, when she was caught up on her work, she would ask if I had any jobs that she could do for me. Sometimes I did, and I knew I could always count on her to do them correctly and promptly. By helping with my tasks, Julie learned more about the organization. The primary function of our department was to provide services to children with disabilities and to their families. Julie became more interested in this over time and played an active and important role in the organization.

"By helping with my tasks, Julie learned more about the organization."

As time went on, we had occasion to talk about our families, and I learned about Julie's parents and her brother, Bill. It was obvious to me that Julie had grown up in a strong Christian family and tried hard to live accordingly.

One day, Julie came to my office door and asked if I had some time to talk to her. Things had been pretty quiet that afternoon, and it was not long before closing time.

I said, "Sure, Julie, come on in."

I called Mary, another secretary, and asked her to cover Julie's desk. Julie and I sat next to a small table in my office. After we chatted for a minute, I asked Julie if there was something that she wanted to share or if there was something that I might help her with.

"Well," she began slowly and in a soft voice, "maybe both. I have been gone from home for a few years. I used to talk to my dad about these things, but I haven't for a while. I respect you and know I can trust you. I need some advice."

"I would be happy to help if I can. Let's give it a try," I said.

"Well," she began again, "You know I have been taking night classes, and there is this guy in my Thursday night psychology class who has offered to help me with my car. You know it's pretty old and not too reliable at times. I really need something better, but I can't afford it."

"Yes, you have told me about your car," I said. "How does this guy fit in?"

"The other night after class I was telling Linda, a girl I sit next to in class, about my car problems, and this guy Randy overheard us talking. He told me he has a brother who has a car dealership about ten miles from campus and that he has some really nice, reliable used cars. He offered to go with me to look at them and see about trading mine in," Julie said.

"I know I shouldn't be...so paranoid."

"It sounds like that might help you out; perhaps you could find something nice you can afford," I said. "But for some reason you sound hesitant."

"Yes, I am," she continued. "This Randy is a nice guy from what little I know of him just from class. But he is quite a bit older than I am, and I am just not sure if this is something I should do. I know I shouldn't be... so paranoid."

"I think I understand what your concern is, Julie," I said. "You don't know if this man is simply interested in helping you with your car problem or if he may have other interests or intentions. And since you don't know him that well, you are not sure you want to take a chance."

"Exactly," she said. "I could use the help, but…"

"Let me suggest a couple of things that you might think about," I said.

"Please do," Julie responded.

"Since you need to take your car to the dealership anyway, you might suggest that you drive separately and meet him there, or you might take this friend Linda or your roommate, Susie, with you to help check out some cars. If Randy is really looking to help you, those options should be fine with

"I think I can work this out and get his help."

him. If not, simply tell him you don't think you are interested and thank him for the offer. You will then know your concerns were likely valid ones."

"Those are good ideas. I just wish I knew him better. I think I can work this out and get his help. Susie loves cars anyway, and she probably would like to go with me."

As we talked a bit more I said, "You know, Julie, I am sure you have been told this many times, but you are a very beautiful young lady. No doubt, you attract men quite easily, probably all kinds of men. That's likely what made you hesitant about Randy. This is not the first time you have had those feelings, right?"

"You are so right!" she said. "And unfortunately, it has become far more than just being hesitant."

"Oh, what do you mean?" I asked.

"This really bothers me a lot," Julie said.

"It's gotten to where I hardly trust any guy anymore," she said. "You would never believe the number of times I have cried myself to sleep, praying that God would put big scars across my face. If He did that, then I would know that someone really cared about me because of who I am, rather than because of what I look like. I am not kidding. I'm telling the truth!"

I knew Julie would not lie to me; I was sure that she was telling the truth, but I certainly was shocked to hear it. Julie knew I was surprised. I thought to myself, "Nobody prays for scars on their face. Whoever heard of that?"

Julie tried to hold back the tears, but by this time they were running down her cheeks. I still was not sure what to say.

Julie went on, "I worked as a waitress in different places during high school and afterward. Then I worked the desk at two different hotels near where I lived. You would not believe some of the things I had to put up with because the men were customers and I had to treat them nicely. I needed the job. I know a lot of guys and have gone out with several. I had a boyfriend for a while. Many of the guys were pretty nice, but some were so unpredictable and often disrespectful. I mean, I had to cut it off right away. You never

"I don't know who I can trust anymore."

know what they want, but I try to be good. I don't know who I can trust any more. The only ones I feel good about are my brother, Bill, and Andy who lived next door when we were kids. Andy is a year older than I am, and he protected me like I was his little sister. But now I just don't know. Like I said, I wish I was not so paranoid."

I guess I finally found some words and I began, "You know, Julie, most people would be jealous of you and simply think you are a very lucky young lady and that you have everything going for you. They would have absolutely no idea that beauty like yours could cause such pain. And I guess that probably includes me. I am really sorry. But I bet you that someday a guy will come along who will see all the beauty inside of you and will be attracted to you for far more than your looks. And I think you will know it when that time comes. He will be a lucky guy. You're a very special young lady, and I am very glad you are now a regular part of our staff. You contribute a lot to this organization."

As Julie left the room, she turned and said, "Thanks. I really like working here and thanks for the help. I think the car thing will work out just fine."

"You are welcome, Julie. I hope it does," I said.

After Julie left my office, I thought about our discussion for a while. I guess I had never looked at beauty from Julie's perspective. She helped me understand it from her point of view.

—————⸺◈⸻—————

Is Julie's case that unusual, or does attractiveness such as hers cause similar problems for many young women? It was obvious to me that her concern was genuine and very personal. It certainly had an effect on how she viewed her relationships with men. Her beauty did not bring her happiness or contentment. Yet, isn't this what we are often lead to believe?

Our society places great emphasis on appearances and external beauty. This has always been true for women, but it is also true for men. Just look at the ads, magazines, television, and, of course, the movies. Notice the mannequins in the department stores. They all project beautiful people.

"True beauty goes much deeper than the surface…"

Are there times when we are disappointed with what we see in the mirror? We need to remember that we are not defined simply by how we look. True beauty goes much deeper than the surface, and good looks do not guarantee love or happiness. External beauty is fleeting and fades with time. However, inner beauty can increase with time as we cultivate our personal qualities. It can last a lifetime.

It is vitally important that we like ourselves as we are and for what we are inside. We must remember that we don't become happy by trying to be like others but by recognizing and appreciating how special and unique we are and by making the most of the many wonderful gifts we have been given.

"We've got this gift of love,

but love is like a precious plant.

You can't just accept it and leave it in

the cupboard or just think it's going to

get on by itself. You've got to keep

watering it. You've got to really look

after it and nurture it."

— John Lennon

...about love

It was a brisk, clear fall morning. Early October in Michigan brings the most beautiful colors, as striking as if they had been painted by an artist. The children had just returned to their classroom from recess. I had been on the playground and had joined them in a game of kick ball, so I was returning to my room also. I was thoroughly enjoying my job as a special education teacher in an elementary school. This group of children remained with me for the entire day, and they had more energy than any class I had ever had. They also were a very caring and considerate group. They were a wonderful class.

About ten minutes into the math assignment for the day, I noticed Tony in the last row. He was not working on his math but was looking out the window with a dazed look on his face. I saw tears in his eyes. Tony had just recently celebrated his eighth birthday, and his dark hair and brown eyes made him quite a handsome boy. Tony was a bit small for an eight-year-old, but the size of his heart made up for his small stature. He was always there to lend a hand or to help another student. He was now in my class for the second year, for often students in special programs remain with the same teacher for two or three years. He was not a slow child, but he did have some unique learning difficulties.

> *"Tony's tears bothered me because he had always been happy, fun loving, and full of energy."*

Tony's tears bothered me because he had always been happy, fun loving, and full of energy. Obviously something was bothering him. As I worked my way to the back of the class, stopping to speak to several other students along my way, I ended up at Tony's desk. Very quietly, so others would not notice, I asked Tony, "Is there something bothering you today, Tony?"

He said, "No."

"Are you sure?" I asked him.

"Yeah, there's nothing wrong."

"Okay, but if by chance you would like to stop in after school for a minute, you are most welcome. I will be here working on some papers, so please come in if you wish,"

I replied. Tony would only talk if others were not present. We'd had some pretty good talks in the past, so I hoped that he might take advantage of my invitation and stop by.

It happened to be a day that I had a meeting across town after school. Since I wanted to give Tony a chance to share what was bothering him, I called ahead to tell the other attendees that they should just go ahead without me since I might be late or may miss the meeting altogether.

Nine minutes after the dismissal bell, Tony stuck his head in my doorway. By that time, almost all of the students had left the building. They leave rather quickly at the end of the day, especially on nice ones.

"Nine minutes after the dismissal bell, Tony stuck his head in my doorway."

Needless to say, I was very glad to see Tony. I invited him in, and we sat in a couple of chairs near my desk. I liked to use this area with students and parents because there were no barriers like the teacher's desk between us when we talked. I wanted Tony to feel comfortable.

Tony sat for a minute, and then I asked him how his day had gone and what his plans were for the evening.

He replied, "Okay at school, but I am really afraid and upset about my mom."

"Tell me why," I encouraged him.

As Tony began, the tears formed again. He began by saying, "Remember I told you that my mom and dad got a divorce about two years ago?"

"Yes," I said. "Your mother and I have talked about it on more than one occasion."

Tony's mother was a bright, hard working and talented woman. She was in her early 30's, and her dark hair and dark eyes made it easy to see the resemblance between mother and son. Tony was an only child.

The divorce had been extremely upsetting for Tony because his dad was a very special person to him. This is most often the case, even when the father has less than desirable qualities and his behavior is largely responsible for the divorce. Children may not understand all the details, but they still love their dads (or moms) very much, even through all the hurting times. When Tony's dad moved to another state with his new girlfriend a short time after the divorce, Tony was simply devastated. He did not hear much from his father after that. Needless to say, this was a difficult and painful loss for him. Tony's mother was well aware of the emptiness Tony had felt. She worked very hard to make his life as normal as possible in spite of her responsibilities and long work hours.

Tony continued on, "I really love my mom very much. She means everything to me. She is my best friend. I tell her everything. We do a lot together." He told me that she had recently met a man and had started to go on dates with him. "He's a nice guy, but I am scared that she will not have much time for me in the future and, even worse, that she will not have as much love for me," he said.

After hesitating, I asked, "Well, why do you think that is true?"

He explained that she was going to be spending more time with her new friend, and if she loved him, there would likely be very little love left for him.

He reasoned, "There is only so much love a person has to give, you know."

As he spoke, it became more clear how he felt and why he was so upset. Other children I had talked to had expressed the same feeling, but Tony was the first to express it so well and so seriously. He really was scared.

It took a minute for me to gather my thoughts, and then I said, "You know, Tony, your mother is a wonderful lady. I have talked to her several times. She really cares about you and loves you very much. I know you love her, and you want her to be happy don't you?"

He answered, "Yes."

"Your mom may meet some men and date. One day she may fall in love with one and want to marry him. Do you think that would be okay?" I asked.

"I guess so," he said.

I went on, "Even if that happens, I bet your mom will still love you as much as she ever has, and that will not change because she gets married."

"Do you really think so? Why?" he asked.

"Well, Tony," I said, "a good counselor friend once told me she did not believe that love is like a pie. She said if love were like a pie, it would be all gone as soon as the person with the pie had given it all away. The pieces would all be gone, and there would be no more."

"Well, isn't that true?" he asked.

In answer to his question I explained, "My friend said,

and I agree with her, that love is more like a water faucet in your house. Love is like the water flowing out. I think it can keep flowing forever and ever and never stop. The only time it would stop would be if the giver wanted to shut it off." Then I added,

> *"Love is like the water flowing out. I think it can keep flowing forever and ever and never stop."*

"I believe the love your mother has for you is like that and that it will always keep on flowing."

"Do you really think so?" Tony asked.

"Sure," I answered. "It will never need to stop. There will always be enough for you and a new husband and for many others who your mother loves and cares about. Do you understand what I mean?"

I felt good inside as he looked up at me with a little smile, wiped the tears from his eyes, and said, "I think I do. I hope you are right about my mom."

"Would you like me to talk to her, Tony?" I asked.

He said, "No, at least not yet. I think I will talk to her about that faucet your friend told you about."

"I bet your mom would like to talk about it with you too," I said.

As we walked to the door, I put my hand on his shoulder and thanked Tony for coming by.

"Have a good evening. See you in the morning," I said.

"Okay, and thanks a lot," Tony replied, as he moved quickly through the halls to get out of school and home. He knew his mom would be waiting for him and probably would be worried.

The next day, Tony seemed fine in school. He did not say anything to me about our talk. Over the next few days, I saw that his behavior was pretty much back to normal. He acted more like the happy-go-lucky kid I knew.

One day the next week, Tony stopped in to see me after school. He said, "You know, my mom and I talked about that faucet idea, and she understood it just like you do. And besides, she told me I was so special to her that she would never shut that faucet off."

"That's great, Tony. I am very happy for you," I said.

⟫◆⟪

As humans, we need others in our lives to be fulfilled. Young or old, we all need love. To give love and to be loved is vital to our existence and happiness.

By nature, the love between a parent and a child is very strong. Most parents would think it unimaginable that their love would ever end. However, we must remember that children may not understand this and may need extra reassurance, especially during times of change or turmoil. We need to let them know our faucets will never run dry.

"No one can make you feel inferior without your consent."

— *Eleanor Roosevelt*

...about confidence

The dust flew like never before. Woody had just slid into second base. I could hardly see him from the sidelines because the dust was so thick for a minute, but he was safe. Talk about a sandlot game, this was one for real. We had a neighborhood ball field that many of us had created on a vacant lot. It was rough, but it was ours, and we were very proud of it. It really was mostly sand. The grass and weeds were all worn down because the field saw a great deal of activity all summer long. Most of the time it was very dry, and after almost every game, we were all pretty filthy and ready for a shower.

Fortunately, there were a lot of kids in our neighborhood. Most of us that played regularly were between seven and fourteen years of age. Woody was eight and I was nine. Being good friends, we always tried to get on the same team for our games, but it did not always work out that way. Woody was pretty good, especially for one of the smaller kids. On this particular day, Woody had played fairly well and had made two hits and scored a run.

Just a few months ago, more than fifty years after our sandlot games, I reconnected with Woody back in our hometown where we grew up. We had been together through high school. Fortunately for both of us, we were able to schedule a time when we could meet for coffee and spend most of the morning together. We talked about the early years in our neighborhood and the years we shared in junior and senior high school. We remembered many fun times and many mutual childhood friends.

"We talked about the early years in our neighborhood and the years we shared in junior and senior high school."

After we had visited for nearly two hours, Woody said, "You know, we had a lot of good times together as kids, but there were a few experiences that were not very pleasant ones. The strange thing is that they may have been minor events, but to me, they were very important, and I still remember them very clearly."

Naturally, being curious about what he was about to say, I asked, "Well, what would those be, Woody?"

"You probably remember how we picked teams to play ball," he began. "A couple of the older kids always seemed to decide that they would be captains, and they would alternate picking players for their teams."

"Sure, I remember that," I responded.

"As you know, very often I was the last kid picked, probably because I was younger and smaller. I remember praying that I would not be the last one picked. It just depended on what other kids were there that day, but often I was last."

"And I remember that did not make you feel too good, did it?" I asked.

"It made me feel terrible. I didn't think I was that bad, but I really felt like I was not worth much and nobody really wanted me on their team," he said.

> *"'I remember praying that I would not be the last one picked.'"*

"It was just your age and size, that's all," I said. "You did play pretty well and got much better as you got older."

"I know, but at the time it was a real let-down. And you know, even in junior high, the same thing happened in gym class. The teacher would often ask two boys to be captains and select teams. I was only a captain once. I wasn't picked last in school quite as much because I was a little better athlete, I guess. But because of my earlier experiences, I felt bad as I watched others who were selected last or nearly last. I saw on their faces the same feeling of inadequacy that I had felt."

"I think you're right. I watched that too. Some of the kids really felt bad," I said. "That was true in school back then, but I think teachers are wiser today and understand much better how simple things like that can have a lasting effect on a youngster. After spending over thirty years in public education, I know a great deal has been learned about self-esteem and confidence in children. That is taken into consideration in education today."

"There is something else from elementary school that I never understood but that has always bothered me too," Woody went on. "Remember the patrol boys?"

"Sure I do," I said.

"Well, I really wanted to be a patrol boy. You know, wear one of those belts with the badge on it and help the kids cross the street. I always thought that was a good job, helping the kids be safe."

"Yes, I know. Were you a patrol boy?" I asked.

"No," he said.

"Why not?" I asked.

"They wouldn't let me. They told me no when I tried," he answered.

"Did they tell you why?" I asked.

"No, I never really found out why. I just always felt that they didn't think I was good enough. You know I wasn't an angel in school, but I thought I was an average kid. I really wanted to be a patrol boy. I thought there was something wrong with me when they said I couldn't," Woody added.

"That's interesting, Woody. I never knew that. I didn't know that was so important to you. I am really surprised that they didn't give you a reason. It seems like that is the least they could have done," I continued.

"It just always stuck with me," Woody said. "I have never forgotten it."

"Isn't it strange, the things we remember and how important they are even many years later?" I asked. "They may have been very minor and not even noticeable to others, but to us they are lasting memories, often with less than positive influences on our lives."

"That's for sure," Woody agreed. "But you haven't heard the one that affected me the most yet."

"What was that, Woody?" I asked.

"Remember Mrs. Larsen and that tenth grade literature class?" he asked. "The one where we were asked to read a section of the story out loud in class?"

"Sure, I remember it. Not my favorite memory of high school but I recall it," I said.

"One day, Mrs. Larsen called on me," Woody began. "I remember it so clearly, even though this was over forty-five years ago. It was a sunny afternoon. I sat in the row by the windows, probably wishing I was outside playing ball or something. Anyway, I began to read out loud. I wasn't doing too badly. Then as I read, the book spoke about these people going through a Polish town. Well, I pronounced the word "Polish" as "polish" like in a shoe shine, you know. The whole class laughed, and I think even the teacher had to hold it back. I was never so embarrassed in my life. I really felt stupid. I read a little more, and then she called on someone else. I couldn't wait to get out of the room that afternoon. I know they probably weren't, but it felt like every kid in the room was looking at me and still laughing. At least, that's how I felt."

"I think you're right," I said. "Nothing seems more devastating at the time than being laughed at by your peers."

"I guess I didn't think about it a lot back then, but I think it really influenced me quite a bit. I know all kids experience some tough times during their school years. I am not sure we really realize the impact they can have on a person," Woody said. "Most of the time, my school years were great fun with lots of good memories, but I do think things like that incident in English class did influence how I felt about myself."

"'...it felt like every kid in the room was looking at me and still laughing.'"

"How was that?" I asked.

"It seems like I just sort of slid through high school, often taking easier classes. I never went near chemistry, physics, or calculus. And I never even had a counselor who talked to me or encouraged me to take other classes and go on to college," he said.

"But I know you went. You started when I did, the fall after we graduated," I said.

"Yes," Woody responded. "But it was sort of an accident."

"How was that?" I asked.

"I had a good job right out of high school. That summer I applied to one college and was accepted. At the last minute, I decided to go."

"Well, I am sure glad you did," I said.

"Me too!" Woody agreed. "But it was not easy. Like I said, I took the easy route in high school, and I was sorry later that I had not worked harder. The main problem, though, was that I was too quiet, pretty insecure, and almost somewhat withdrawn in my college classes. I really lacked confidence in myself and rarely spoke up in class. As you know, that certainly does not help your grades any. The professors want you to speak up and act interested."

"No kidding," I said, "I know just what you mean."

Woody went on, "I could have done so much better in college, and it would have been so much easier if I'd have had just a little more courage and confidence in myself."

"You are probably right," I said. "But you ended up doing very well and being quite successful from what I know."

"Yes," he said. "After a lot of hard work, I ended up with four degrees. In another year, I will be retiring as an assistant professor at the university. My career has been very rewarding. One thing that I have always tried to be is helpful and supportive to any of my students who seemed to be less confident or seemed somewhat withdrawn. Maybe those experiences years ago helped me to be a bit more understanding and patient with some of my students."

"'Those experiences… helped me to be a bit more understanding and patient with some of my students.'"

"I am sure they did, Woody," I agreed. "I bet you have been a great professor, and the students have enjoyed having you."

"I hope so," he replied. "I really worked hard at it, but I also loved it."

As the time drew close to noon, we were both surprised that we had talked so long. We'd had a great time.

"Thanks for listening," Woody said. "I have not shared most of that with anyone, but you can see how it has been just under the surface for a long time."

"You're welcome," I said. "I am glad you shared those things with me, and I sure am happy that we had this chance to get together."

As we said good bye, we made plans to meet again. We still had many more stories to tell and experiences to share about when we were kids.

⇒•◇•⇐

After we had parted, I thought about how many times the things that happen to us have an adverse effect on us. This includes the negative behavior of others towards us, even when it's not intentional. At the time, the events may seem minor or not even noticeable to others, but to us they are very important and influential. If only we were more able to learn from it, let go of it, and move on with our lives. Too often, however, these experiences may stay with us for years.

Our lives today, including our self-esteem and our feelings of self-worth, are largely a result of the experiences we have had in our youth. Was that environment a negative one, or was it a positive and nurturing one?

Walking back to my car, I reflected on how great it would be if we could learn to not personalize and internalize every unpleasant thing that happens to us. If we could manage that, we could utilize and maximize our true self-worth.

"Fall seven times,

stand up eight."

— *Japanese Proverb*

...about determination

It was a beautiful summer afternoon and the skies were as clear as I had ever seen them. Mary sat on the soft, thick grass near the edge of the track. She was so exhausted that she could hardly speak. The temperature had risen to the mid 80's as the track and field events continued into early afternoon. I was attending the state-level summer Special Olympics held at a nearby university. Mary had just completed the 100 meter race.

Many volunteer "huggers" attended these Special Olympic events. One of their main functions was to pick an athlete and meet that person at the end of the race. Sandy was Mary's hugger. She was majoring in special education at the university. She was excited about the profession and took advantage of every opportunity to become involved with young people with disabilities. She had both energy and enthusiasm.

As I crossed the track and walked toward Mary, I saw that Sandy had met her and was congratulating and comforting her. Sandy was taking deep breaths along with Mary, as though that might help Mary catch her breath.

Mary looked up and smiled when she saw me coming. Still trying to catch her breath, she said, "Hi, I'm so glad you came to watch us today."

"Hi, Mary, I am really happy that I could be here to see you participate," I replied.

Over several years, I had supported the Special Olympics and made an effort to attend events whenever I could. Usually, I attended the basketball games or track and field events. Most of the time, participants included students who were in school programs for which I had administrative and supervisory responsibilities. The teachers, paraprofessionals, coaches, and volunteers always did a superb job with the participants.

It was very rewarding to see the sheer determination exhibited by the young people participating at the Special Olympics. While they were competing, they were having the times of their lives. It did not matter if it was an individual or a team event. The smiles on their faces always made it clear that they were thoroughly enjoying themselves. Their enthusiasm seemed endless.

As Sandy put her arm around Mary, it looked like Mary was finally catching her breath. After another minute or two, Mary turned to me and asked, "Did you see me run?"

"Yes, I did. You ran quite a race, Mary," I answered.

Mary said, "Well, I did run fast and did my best, but I did trip a couple of times."

"You never really lose unless you don't get up."

I knew this because I had watched the entire race and had seen Mary stumble down onto the track twice. She had pulled herself together, gotten back up, and kept on running. She finished the race last, but it did my heart good to see her have the gumption to get up and continue each time.

I said, "Mary, I was very glad to see you get back up each time and go on to finish the race."

She took another deep breath, looked at both Sandy and me again with a smile, and said, "Well, you know, you never really lose unless you don't get up."

We both agreed with her, and Sandy said, "You are absolutely right, Mary."

What a wonderful attitude! I have never forgotten that day. Mary ran in four events that day and she completed every event. She had learned to give each one of them everything she had and to do her very best. She did not receive any medals that day. Perhaps next year she would do better, but she knew she had trained a lot and worked very hard for this day. She knew she had given her best, and she was happy with that. Mary did not lose that day.

This is not a success story like that of the fabulous Wilma Rudolph, an Olympic track star. Wilma grew up wearing braces on her legs because of polio. One day she took the braces off, began to walk, then run, then train and eventually became a track star. Wilma later was an Olympic champion, winning three gold medals in track events at the 1960 Olympics in Rome. What a great story!

Mary was simply a young lady from a small farming community in central Michigan. She attended special education programs until she graduated from high school. She learned early on that she had to work very hard to overcome and compensate for the areas where she was a bit less capable. She helps us remember what we all know but often forget, that there is no such thing as failure unless we choose to not keep on trying. Mary's determination continued as she worked and trained very hard. The following year she did win a medal, and the next year she won a GOLD medal!

⇒◆⇐

One quality that I have seen time and again among young people with disabilities is determination. This is true not only in sports and Special Olympic events, but in many everyday activities. They simply don't give up. They continue in a definitive, firm, and persistent direction toward their goals. We can all learn from them and from the heart they put into whatever they do.

" ...transplants are a great step forward in science's service of man...and organ donation is a genuine act of love. "

— *Pope John Paul II*

...about making a difference

As I listened carefully, he continued to speak softly. He sat on the edge of the chair, and as he spoke, tears welled up in his eyes. Mark was sharing with me the story of the recent, tragic death of his teenaged son, Steve.

One weekend a year, I speak to a group of men at a religious retreat center. After my talk, I am given a small office to use in case any of the men would like to privately share their thoughts with me or to ask any questions. My main role is simply to listen, not to give guidance or advice. Usually five or six of the men stop by to talk.

Mark was the first person to stop in and see me that afternoon. In my talk, I had spoken of the loss of our daughter Denise to a five year battle with cancer. I had shared some of my experiences, as well as my feelings and emotions during her illness and death and the time following.

Mark began, "I connected with you immediately when you spoke of losing your daughter. I just recently lost my teenaged son in a terrible automobile accident."

His voice shook somewhat as he continued to tell me the story, and he began to cry. As I listened to what he said, I felt very bad for him and his recent loss.

A friend once said to me after the sudden death of his son, "We now belong to the same fraternity."

That is how I felt about Mark. We had both experienced what I believe to be the most tragic loss a parent could possibly endure. We talked a bit more about our children and our losses; I watched and listened. Mark began to tell me how, at the last possible moment, he had decided to donate his son's organs. This act required the permission of both the father and the mother. Mark was divorced and his former wife was living in South America. Fortunately, Mark was able to reach her and receive her permission for the donation.

As Mark continued, his voice became more smooth and clear, and his face and eyes began to change. A little smile came to his face, and his eyes brightened. Mark told me that he had received information from his local organ procurement organization about the people who received his son's organs. Of course, he was not given specific identifying information, but he was told how the organs had benefited these many people.

At this point in his story, Mark actually had a big smile on his face.

"A middle-aged father out there no longer needs to go on dialysis every week. That man is healthy and living with one of my son's kidneys. Sometimes, I stop and wonder if the mother I see walking down the street with her three children is the woman that now has Steve's heart beating in her chest. That young mother," he explained, "had only a very short time to live. Now she enjoys a normal life with a strong young heart inside of her."

> *"That man is healthy and living with one of my son's kidneys."*

Mark went on to describe several of the other recipients. Nearly fifty people may have benefited from the donations of his son. As Mark spoke of the benefits of organ and tissue donations, I developed an entirely new appreciation for the importance of this gift.

It's clear to see that Mark was very proud of the decision he had made to donate his son's organs and tissues. This had to have been one of the most traumatic, devastating and emotional times of his life, but Mark had the ability to make this very unselfish decision that would bring positive, life-long changes to the lives of so many. He knows a part of his son still lives on to help others.

⟽⟶◆⟵⟾

Mark taught me much in the short time we spent together. He called my attention to a topic about which I knew very little. I decided to increase my awareness and learn more about the benefits of organ and tissue donations. I contacted the Gift of Life Michigan Organ and Tissue Donation Program and was able to meet with members of a couple of donor families. Family members talked about the difficult time they went through when they lost their loved one. At the same time, they shared how they were comforted knowing that the donations could help another family from experiencing a similar loss. They were consoled by knowing that part of their loved one continued to live.

"A part of his son still lives on to help others."

Not only is there comfort to the donor family, but it certainly is a blessing and a special gift to the recipient and his or her family.

My contacts with the Gift of Life have been very pleasant and helpful. I was able to visit and tour their facilities, and one of the coordinators gave me a thorough explanation of their programs and services. This is a fascinating agency with services that are provided by very dedicated professionals.

"What better gift could we give than to leave a part of ourselves?"

It appears that the number of organ transplants is increasing, along with the number of people registering for organ donations. However, the number of waiting recipients continues to grow even more rapidly.

Thousands of people are alive and healthy today because of these generous donations which can change and save people's lives. Recipients say they have a new lease on life. Donors are generous people, generous enough to help save the lives of people they don't even know. What better gift could we give than to leave a part of ourselves? Doing so is the final way you and I are capable of making a significant difference.

"Reflect on your present blessings,

of which every man has many;

not on your past misfortunes,

of which all men have some."

— *Charles Dickens*

…reflection

I have spent many hours in the woods of northern Michigan. The lovely streams and rivers have always fascinated me, both as a child and as an adult. I enjoy just sitting and watching the water flow. In some places, it moves rapidly, and in others, it moves hardly at all. I particularly love hearing the water tumble over the rocks. It's beautiful music to my ears.

Sometimes, I'll toss a twig into the water and watch it float downstream. I remember watching one twig sail smoothly along until it suddenly bumped into a large rock. It was caught for a while, but eventually the current moved it around the rock, and it continued on its way. Another twig's journey was interrupted when it was pulled under water in a turbulent spot. I didn't see it for a while, and I thought it was gone for good, but then it resurfaced and floated into calmer water. I will often watch the twigs until they're out of sight, wondering where their voyages will finally end.

Our lives are similar to these twigs' journeys. Much of the time, we go through life uneventfully, but then we bump into an obstacle. It may stop us temporarily, but then the currents of life and time gently move us on. Also, there are times when life's burdens will almost sink us, but just as the twig resurfaced, we too must rise up and trust that smoother times lie ahead.

Smooth water is quiet. The rocks in the stream are what make the water sparkle and sing. Likewise, the challenges in our lives add interest and force us to grow. The final outcomes may not always be easy, but they build character and understanding. Afterward, we can use the knowledge we have gained to help others who are facing similar circumstances. No one likes difficult times, but they do have value. We could not have the same appreciation for our good times if we had smooth sailing throughout our lives.

I hope you will enjoy the routine times in your life. I also hope that you will take special note of the wonderful, exciting times, celebrating them with gusto. And finally, I hope the turbulent times that you face will be few and far between. But remember, water's beautiful music would not exist without the rocks that lie within the stream.

May the lessons you have learned and the strength you have gained on your journey sustain you until calm returns.

Enjoy love, laughter, good health, joy, and peace …always.

— Harry

" The days come and go,

but they say nothing. And if we do not

use the gifts they bring, they carry them

as silently away. "

— *Ralph Waldo Emerson*

Resources

Want to Know More?

If you are interested in learning more about adoption, hunger, hospice, or organ and tissue donation, the following resources offer a beginning for you:

...about adoption

World Association for Children & Parents (WACAP)

P.O. Box 88948
Seattle, WA 98138

800-732-1887
206-575-4550

http://www.wacap.org

...about hunger

Bread for the World

1100 Wayne Avenue, Suite 1000
Silver Spring, MD 20910

301-608-2400

http://www.bread.org

Food for the Poor, Inc.

550 SW 12th Ave., Dept. 9662
Deerfield Beach, FL 33442

800-427-9104
800-401-4974
954-427-2222

http://www.foodforthepoor.org

...about mortality (hospice)

HOSPICE FOUNDATION OF AMERICA

1621 Connecticut Ave., NW, Suite 300
Washington, DC 20009

800-854-3402 (phone)
202-638-5312 (fax)

http://www.hospicefoundation.org

NATIONAL HOSPICE & PALLIATIVE CARE ORGANIZATION (NHPCO)

1700 Diagonal Road, Suite 625
Alexandria, VA 22314

703-837-1500 (phone)
703-837-1233 (fax)

http://www.nhpco.org

...about making a difference (organ and tissue donation)

COALITION ON DONATION

700 North 4th Street
Richmond, VA 23219

804-782-4920 (phone)
804-782-4643 (fax)

http://www.donatelife.net
E-mail: coalition@donatelife.net

UNITED NETWORK FOR ORGAN SHARING

P.O. Box 2484
Richmond, VA 23218

804-782-4800
804-782-4817

http://www.unos.org

GIFT OF LIFE MICHIGAN

2203 Platt Road
Ann Arbor, MI 48104

800-482-4881

http://www.tsm-giftoflife.org

ABOUT THE AUTHOR

Harry Grether has enjoyed a successful career as a public school teacher and administrator. His vast experiences in the areas of personnel and human relations as well as in the field of disabilities have provided him with much to share with others.

Though his family is an important priority, he also spends time writing, speaking, and volunteering for hospice. He enjoys golf and other outdoor activities such as fishing, bicycling, and snowmobiling. He lives in Midland, Michigan with his wife, Helen.

Visit Harry Grether at www.harrygrether.com
or contact him at hgrether@chartermi.net

LESSONS FROM
AN IMPERFECT WORLD

BY HARRY J. GRETHER

CHECK YOUR LOCAL BOOKSTORE, OR ORDER USING THE INFORMATION BELOW.

Visit www.harrygrether.com and use the online order form, or send your order via U.S. Mail and include the following information (please print):

1. Number of books *($14.00 each; tax included)*

2. Address where to send the book(s)

3. Check or money order (in U.S. funds) for full amount
   (please include $2.00 shipping and handling for each book)

ORDERS MAY BE MAILED TO:

~~Rising Sun Venture Productions (or RSVP)~~
~~P.O. Box 1295~~
Midland, MI 48641-1295

Harry Grether, com

YOUR COPIES WILL BE SIGNED BY THE AUTHOR IF YOU SO REQUEST.

ALSO, if you wish it as a gift, include who it is for, a special note to be written in the book by the author, and the address where it is to be sent.

THANK YOU FOR YOUR ORDER!

Harry Grether may be reached at hgrether@chartermi.net or at RSVP

harrygrether@gmail.com